Rachel's
Favourite
Food at home

Collins

Rachel's Favourite Food at home

Rachel Allen

I dedicate this book to my husband, Isaac, whose love, wisdom and inspiration I could not live without.

First published in 2006 by Collins,
an imprint of HarperCollins Publishers Ltd.
77–85 Fulham Palace Road
London W6 8JB

The Collins website address is: www.collins.co.uk

Collins is a registered trademark of HarperCollins Publishers Ltd.

09 08 07

9 8 7 6

A catalogue record for this book is available from the British Library.

Senior Commissioning Editor: Jenny Heller
Managing Editor: Emma Callery
Editors: Gillian Haslam & Alastair Laing
Design: Smith & Gilmour, London
Location photography: Cristian Barnett
Food photography: Peter Cassidy
Food and Props Stylist: Felicity Barnum-Bobb

ISBN-10 0 00 724232 8
ISBN-13 978 0 00 724232 0

Colour reproduction by Colourscan, Singapore
Printed and bound by Lego, Italy

Contents

Introduction

I think my very earliest memory of food (actually, probably my earliest memory of anything) is of my sister, Simone, feeding me mashed banana as though I were her baby. She's four years older than me and as she was probably only about five or six at the time, I was only about two! Then, when we were a bit older, we loved helping mum in the kitchen (although now I can imagine that we were probably not that much help), and would often bake cakes and biscuits ourselves. We were very lucky that there was always good home-cooked food in the house, even when Mum was working, and we always sat down at the table together as a family and enjoyed great chats. Often there would be friends there too. It is still the same when I stay with my parents in Dublin.

So now that I have children myself, cooking at home is very important to me. It evokes such happy childhood memories. I also love that time of the evening when my husband, Isaac, gets home from work and we have a glass of wine in the kitchen while one of us prepares supper. This is our time for catching up on what's been going on during the day. Of course, there is the added pleasure of our children's company – even if they are fighting!

Many of you may be parents, and working ones at that, so I have included plenty of suggestions in this book for easy meals that all the family can enjoy. Even better, they can be whipped up in no time. But there is so much more to enjoying cooking at home, like those times when you are looking forward to friends or family coming to stay, or when you're planning a big party for a special occasion, or when it's such a glorious day that you decide to have a spontaneous lunchtime barbecue or a little alfresco dinner party on a balmy evening. There are also those important times when only mum's cooking will do – I know that's how I feel about my own mum's food, and hopefully my children will feel the same about mine. You may want to bake a gorgeous cake or some buns for that special somebody on a special day, or even make completely delicious edible gifts. Cooking great food at home is a joy that I wish to pass along to you. Among the many recipes in this book I hope there is inspiration aplenty, and that this book will become a much-loved member of your family. May it last you many happy years, and feed you many joyous meals!

1 Easy Family Food

I love family meals since this is when everyone gets to sit together and talk about what went on during the day. This type of food should be easy to prepare and quick to rustle up, or else made in advance earlier in the day. This is simple food that the whole family will enjoy and the recipes can be easily amended to suit everyone's taste.

Scrambled Eggs with Tomato, Chilli and Coriander

SERVES 2 / VEGETARIAN

I love this scrambled egg variation, which I first tasted in a restaurant looking out over Mexico City. It's full of protein (from the eggs) and antioxidants (from the coriander), and is a great way to start the day. Of course, you can omit the chilli for children, the coriander still makes it special.

15g (½oz) butter
1 ripe tomato, finely chopped
½–1 chilli, deseeded and finely chopped (optional for children)
4 free-range eggs, best quality possible
3 tbsp milk
Salt and freshly ground black pepper
1 tbsp chopped fresh coriander

Melt the butter in a saucepan, add the tomato and chilli and cook for a few minutes until the tomato is just softening. Meanwhile, whisk the eggs with the milk and a pinch of salt and pepper. Add to the saucepan and stir gently until the egg is softly scrambled. Stir in the chopped coriander, and serve.

Fruity Breakfast Muffins

MAKES 12 / VEGETARIAN

These are gorgeous muffins and they make delicious breakfast fare. The best thing about this basic recipe is that you can add whatever fruit you like.

2 eggs
100ml (3½fl oz) milk
100ml (3½fl oz) natural yoghurt
75ml (2¾fl oz) sunflower oil
1 tsp vanilla extract
225g (8oz) plain flour
3 tsp baking powder

¼ tsp baking soda
¼ tsp salt
½ tsp ground cinnamon
100g (4oz) wholemeal plain flour
100g (4oz) brown sugar, plus 1–2 tbsp
    brown sugar, for sprinkling (optional)

Preheat the oven to 180°C (350°F), Gas mark 4. Line a muffin tray with 12 muffin cases. Break the eggs into a large mixing bowl and whisk to break up. Whisk in the milk, yoghurt, oil and vanilla. Add the chopped fruit and stir.

In another bowl sift the plain flour, baking powder, baking soda, salt and cinnamon. Add the wholemeal flour and sugar, and mix. Fold the dry ingredients into the wet ingredients. Stop mixing as soon as it comes together, do not over-stir.

Divide the mixture between the muffin cases, sprinkle the tops with brown sugar, if using, and cook in the preheated oven for 20–25 minutes, or until the tops spring back when gently touched. Allow to stand in the tin for 1–2 minutes, then transfer to a wire rack to cool.

RACHEL'S HANDY TIP
If your children won't eat a whole muffin, you can make these in a normal-sized bun tray. If you halve the recipe, you will get 12 buns. Bake for 11–13 minutes.

VARIATIONS

PEACH OR PEACH AND BANANA MUFFINS
Add 2 peaches that have been stoned and chopped into about 5mm–1cm (¼–½in) cubes after you have whisked in the milk, yoghurt, oil and vanilla. For yet more variety replace half the chopped peach with one mashed banana.

APPLE AND CINNAMON MUFFINS

These are so yummy, the cooking apple works better than plain eating apple. Add 250g (9oz) grated, unpeeled cooking apple as for the peach variation.

RHUBARB AND GINGER MUFFINS

These are great as you can use frozen rhubarb. Use 250g (9oz) trimmed, finely chopped (5mm(¼in)) rhubarb in place of the peach, plus 1 generous teaspoon finely grated ginger (whisked in with the wet ingredients).

BERRY MUFFINS

Fresh of frozen berries are delicious in muffins. It's a great way to get children to eat fruit! Use 250g (9oz) berries, such as raspberries, blueberries or blackberries.

Chicken, Ginger and Cashew Stir-fry with Coconut Noodles

SERVES 4-6

This delicious and easy stir-fry is very quick to prepare for both friends and family; it is a favourite of ours and makes a yummy and healthy supper. If you do not have a wok, use a large, heavy bottomed frying pan.

FOR THE NOODLES:
1 litre (1¾ pints) vegetable (or chicken) stock
1 x 410g tin coconut milk
450g (1lb) thin egg noodles

FOR THE STIR-FRY:
2 tbsp sesame oil
1 tbsp sunflower oil
6 large garlic cloves, peeled and finely chopped
1 tbsp finely grated ginger

450g (1lb) chicken, cut into thin strips
1 carrot, peeled, cut in half lengthways and very thinly sliced at an angle
150g (5oz) mangetout, cut in half at an angle
250g (9oz) mushrooms, sliced
150g (5oz) unsalted cashew nuts or peanuts, toasted and roughly chopped
3 tbsp chopped coriander
Salt and freshly ground black pepper

First, prepare the coconut noodles. Place the stock and coconut milk in a saucepan and bring to the boil. Add the noodles and cook according to the instructions on the packet. When cooked, drain. To prevent them from sticking together, add a couple of tablespoonfuls of the cooking liquid to the noodles. Cover and keep warm.

Meanwhile, heat a wok until almost smoking, add the sesame and sunflower oils and the garlic and ginger. Cook for a few seconds, then add the chicken and cook for a few minutes, stirring regularly, until the outside is just golden. Add the carrots, mangetout and mushrooms, toss and stir for another few minutes until the vegetables are just cooked but still slightly crunchy. Toss in the nuts and chopped coriander and season. Serve on top of the noodles.

Broccoli Soup with Parmesan Toasts

SERVES 6-8 / VEGETARIAN

I adore this delicious and nutritious soup. It's great either for family suppers or for a dinner party. The soup can be frozen and the Parmesan toasts prepared in advance, then grilled at the last moment. Ideal if you need a meal in an instant.

FOR THE SOUP:
25g (1oz) butter
2 potatoes, peeled and finely chopped
1 large onion, peeled and chopped
Salt and freshly ground black pepper
1 head of broccoli, with stalk
800ml-1 litre (1¼-1¾ pints) hot vegetable (or chicken) stock
175ml (6fl oz) double cream

FOR THE PARMESAN TOASTS:
8 slices good-quality white bread
75g (3oz) Parmesan cheese, finely grated

Melt the butter in a medium to large saucepan, and add the potatoes and onion, salt and pepper. Cover with a piece of butter wrapper or greaseproof paper and sweat over a gentle heat for 10 minutes.

Meanwhile, cut the broccoli florets from the stalk. Using a small knife, remove the outer layer of skin from the stalk and discard, then chop the stalk into 1cm (½in) pieces. Add to the onion and potato, and sweat for a further 5 minutes.

Add the hot stock to the potatoes, onion and broccoli stalk, bring up to the boil, then add the chopped florets. Boil without the lid over a high heat for 4-5 minutes until soft, then add the cream. Remove from the heat, liquidise and season to taste.

To make the Parmesan toasts, toast the bread on both sides, sprinkle with grated Parmesan and pop under a hot grill or into a hot oven for 2 minutes or until the cheese melts. Cut the toast into fingers and serve on the side with the soup.

Risotto Verde
SERVES 6 / VEGETARIAN

This is a gorgeous, fresh tasting green risotto and is easy to make as it is baked in the oven.

4 tbsp olive oil
250g (9oz) peas, fresh or frozen
100g (4oz) spinach
950ml (1 pint 12fl oz) vegetable (or chicken) stock
1 onion, peeled and finely chopped
2 garlic cloves, peeled and crushed
Salt and freshly ground black pepper
350g (12oz) risotto rice, such as arborio or carnaroli
150ml (5fl oz) white wine
12 stalks of asparagus, ends trimmed and cut in half lengthways
100g (4oz) Parmesan cheese to serve

Preheat the oven to 180°C (350°F), Gas mark 4. On the hob, heat half the olive oil in an ovenproof saucepan, add the peas and spinach and cook, stirring all the time, for 2 minutes, until the spinach wilts. Add about 50ml (2fl oz) of the stock and purée in a blender or food processor. Set aside.

In the same saucepan, heat the remaining olive oil, add the onion and garlic and season with salt and pepper. Cover with a lid and sweat over a gentle heat until soft but not coloured. Add the risotto rice and stir it around in the saucepan for a minute, then add the remaining stock and the wine. Stir and bring it up to the boil, cover with the lid and place in the preheated oven for 15–20 minutes or until the rice is just cooked and all the liquid has been absorbed. Stir in the vegetable purée and set aside with the lid on.

Bring a saucepan of water up to the boil, add a good pinch of salt and the asparagus. Boil for 2–3 minutes or until it is just tender, then drain. Serve the risotto in warm bowls with the asparagus and Parmesan arranged on top.

RACHEL'S HANDY TIP
The alcohol in the wine burns off during cooking and the flavour is lovely, but if you do not want to use it, just replace it with extra stock.

Pasta with Spinach, Bacon and Parmesan

SERVES 4

This is a delicious and super-quick recipe. A firm family favourite!

400g (14oz) spaghetti or tagliatelle
2 tbsp olive oil
125g (4½oz) bacon rashers (10 streaky rashers or 5 back rashers), chopped
2-3 garlic cloves, peeled and finely chopped
150g (5oz) baby spinach leaves
Salt and freshly ground black pepper
50g (2oz) Parmesan cheese, or something similar, freshly grated, to serve

Put a large saucepan of water on to boil and add 1 teaspoon salt. When boiling, add the pasta, stir well and cook rapidly until al dente.

While the pasta is cooking, heat the oil in a large frying pan, add the bacon and garlic and cook on a high heat for about 4 minutes until the bacon is golden and slightly crispy. Add the spinach and stir until it has wilted. Season to taste.

Drain the pasta when cooked and return to the large saucepan. Pour in the bacon and spinach and stir to mix. Serve immediately with the grated cheese.

Creamy Pasta with Sun-blush Tomatoes, Olives and Pine Nuts

SERVES 4-6 / VEGETARIAN

I like to use semi-sun-dried tomatoes for this simple dish, as they are milder and more juicy than the completely sun-dried ones. Leave out the olives if your children don't care for them.

400g (14oz) dried pasta
250ml (8fl oz) crème fraîche
75g (3oz) semi-sun-dried (also called 'sun-blushed') tomatoes
1 tbsp tomato purée
12–16 black olives, pitted and chopped
50g (2oz) pine nuts, toasted in a dry pan until golden
50g (2oz) Parmesan cheese, finely grated
Salt and freshly ground black pepper
Pinch of sugar (optional)

Bring a large saucepan of water with 1 teaspoon salt up to the boil, and cook the pasta according to the instructions on the packet.

Meanwhile, place the crème fraîche in a saucepan and heat to a gentle simmer. Add the sun-blush tomatoes, tomato purée, chopped olives, most of the toasted pine nuts and most of the grated cheese. Season with salt and pepper and taste – it might need a pinch of sugar too.

When the pasta is cooked, drain, leaving a couple of tablespoons of the cooking water with the pasta. Stir in the hot sun-blush tomato sauce, taste and season again if necessary. Sprinkle with the remaining pine nuts and grated Parmesan cheese and serve.

RACHEL'S HANDY TIP
Try drizzling Basil Pesto (see page 217) over this dish. It's also good with slices of chorizo sausage that have been cooked in a hot dry pan for a minute.

Spicy Salmon Cakes

This foolproof recipe makes about 12 salmon cakes for a family supper. You can also use this recipe to make about 40 mini salmon cakes for small bites to serve with drinks for an informal party. They are absolutely delicious served with flavoured mayonnaise (see page 216) and Tomato and Cucumber Salsa (see page 139). Again, if your children do not eat spicy food, you can omit the chilli or Tabasco.

350g (12oz) filleted and skinned salmon, roughly chopped
50g (2oz) butter
2-3 garlic cloves, peeled and crushed
100g (4oz) white breadcrumbs
1 egg, whisked
2 tsp Dijon mustard
2 tbsp lemon juice
2 tbsp chopped coriander (you can chop the small stalks too)
6 spring onions, chopped
2 tsp Worcestershire sauce
1-2 tsp Tabasco sauce or 1 deseeded and chopped chilli (optional for children)

Combine all the ingredients in a food processor and whiz to combine. Taste for seasoning, add more salt, pepper, lemon juice or Tabasco, if necessary. If you do not have a food processor, chop up the salmon as finely as possible and mix together all the ingredients in a bowl. Shape into patties with a 7.5cm (3in) diameter, or 4cm (1½in) diameter patties for mini salmon cakes. Pan-fry in 3-4 tablespoons olive oil on a medium heat for 3-4 minutes on each side (2-3 minutes for mini cakes), or until golden. Serve on warm plates.

VARIATION
This is also delicious with a Mediterranean twist. Omit the Tabasco or chilli and substitute the same amount of basil for the coriander in the salmon cakes, the mayonnaise and salsa.

Pan-fried Mackerel with Herb Butter

SERVES 4 AS A MAIN COURSE OR 8 AS A STARTER

Mackerel is a delicious and healthy fish. It is also serious brain food for children and adults alike. Mackerel is in season from late spring through the summer into September.

FOR THE MACKEREL:
8 fillets of mackerel, with the skins on
75g (3oz) plain flour, seasoned with salt and pepper
25g (1oz) butter, softened
Lemon wedges, to serve
FOR THE HERB BUTTER:
100g (4oz) butter
2 tbsp chopped fresh herbs
1 tbsp lemon juice

First, make the herb butter. Cream the butter in a bowl, add the chopped herbs and the lemon juice. Roll into a sausage shape and wrap in greaseproof paper or cling film. Put into the freezer to chill quickly.

Place a frying pan or a grill-pan on the heat and wait for it to get very hot. When the pan is hot, dip the fillets of fish in the seasoned flour and shake off the excess. Spread the flesh side (not the skin side) with a little soft butter and place butter-side-down on the hot pan. Cook for a couple of minutes, until crisp and golden, then turn over and cook the other side for another 2–3 minutes, turning down the heat if the pan is getting too hot. Serve on hot plates with one or two slices of herb butter slowly melting on the fish, and a wedge of lemon on the side.

Upside-down Rhubarb and Ginger Cake

SERVES 8 / VEGETARIAN

This recipe and the variation opposite are great topsy-turvy puddings and they are wonderfully easy because they are made in a frying pan instead of a cake tin. When I made this for one of my television programmes, the film crew declared it to be the best thing ever!

50g (2oz) butter
250g (9oz) brown sugar
350g (12oz) rhubarb, trimmed and cut
    into 2cm (3/4in) chunks
200g (7oz) plain flour
1 tsp baking powder
1/2 tsp salt

1/4 tsp bicarbonate of soda
2 eggs
200ml (7fl oz) buttermilk or sour milk
75ml (23/4fl oz) vegetable or
    sunflower oil
1 generous tsp of grated ginger

Preheat the oven to 180°C (350°F), Gas mark 4. Melt the butter in a medium-sized ovenproof frying pan (measuring 25cm (10in) in diameter). Stir in half the sugar and cook over a gentle heat for about 2 minutes. Add the rhubarb – there's no need to stir – and remove from the heat and set aside.

Sieve the flour, baking powder, salt and bicarbonate of soda into a bowl. Whisk the eggs in a measuring jug or small bowl and add the remaining sugar, buttermilk, oil and ginger. Mix together, then pour into the dry ingredients and whisk to form a liquid batter. Pour this over the rhubarb in the pan. Place the pan in the oven and bake for 30 minutes or until the cake feels firm in the centre.

Cool for 5 minutes before turning out by placing an inverted plate over the top of the pan and turning pan and plate over together in one quick movement. Serve warm or at room temperature with softly whipped cream.

Upside-down Apple and Cinnamon Cake

SERVES 8 / VEGETARIAN

This variation on the upside-down theme is a perfect end to a special family meal or dinner party. If you have any left over (I certainly never do!), have it with a cup of tea the next day.

50g (2oz) butter
250g (9oz) brown sugar
3 eating apples, peeled, cored
    and sliced 5mm (1/4in) thick
200g (7oz) plain flour
1 tsp baking powder
1/2 tsp salt

1/4 tsp bicarbonate of soda
1 generous tsp ground cinnamon
2 eggs
200ml (7fl oz) buttermilk or sour milk
75ml (23/4fl oz) vegetable
    or sunflower oil

Preheat the oven to 180°C (350°F), Gas mark 4. Melt the butter in a medium-sized ovenproof frying pan (measuring 25cm (10in) in diameter). Stir in half the sugar and cook over a gentle heat for about 2 minutes. Add the apple – there's no need to stir – and remove from the heat and set aside.

Sieve the flour, baking powder, salt, bicarbonate of soda and ground cinnamon into a bowl. Whisk the eggs in a measuring jug or small bowl and add the remaining sugar, buttermilk and oil. Mix together, then pour into the dry ingredients and whisk to combine into a liquid batter. Pour this over the apple in the pan. Place the pan in the preheated oven and bake for 30 minutes or until the cake feels firm in the centre.

Cool for 5 minutes before turning out by placing an inverted plate over the top of the pan and turning pan and plate over together in one quick movement. Serve warm or at room temperature with softly whipped cream.

Toffee Sundae

MAKES 500ML (18FL OZ) / VEGETARIAN

My boys and I all love making sundaes. They're a serious treat! The toffee sauce is the best ever, and keeps for months in the fridge. It's especially delicious for drizzling over ice cream. This recipe makes quite a lot, but since it keeps for so long it's great to have some just waiting for an excuse to be used up.

FOR THE TOFFEE SAUCE:
100g (4oz) butter
175g (6oz) brown sugar
100g (4oz) caster sugar
275g (10oz) golden syrup
250ml (8fl oz) single cream
½ tsp vanilla extract

FOR THE SUNDAE:
1 tub vanilla ice cream
TO SERVE:
Pieces of Heavenly Fudge
  (see page 190) (optional)

For the toffee sauce, put all the ingredients into a saucepan, and boil for about 4–5 minutes, until the sauce is smooth, stirring regularly.

Place a scoop or two of vanilla ice cream in each bowl or glass. Drizzle over the warm toffee sauce and, if you like, crumble two or three pieces of Heavenly Fudge (see page 190) over each bowl and eat!

No-pastry Pear and Almond Tart

SERVES 6 / VEGETARIAN

This is a delicious tart and is also perfect for people who don't want to make pastry. You can use a variety of fruit for the filling (see below).

175g (6oz) icing sugar
50g (2oz) plain flour
100g (4oz) ground almonds
Finely grated zest of 1 lemon
5 egg whites
175g (6oz) butter, melted

2 ripe pears, peeled, cored and
    quartered, then cut into long slices
    about 5mm (1/4in) thick
25g (1oz) flaked almonds
Icing sugar, to serve

Preheat the oven to 200°C (400°F), Gas mark 6. Lightly grease the sides of a 23cm (9in) tart tin with a removable bottom and place a disc of greaseproof paper on the base. If you prefer, you can serve this tart on the tart tin base, in which case do not use a disc of paper.

Sieve the icing sugar and flour into a bowl and stir in the ground almonds and lemon zest. Whisk the egg whites for 30 seconds, until just frothy, and add to the dry ingredients with the warm melted butter. Mix until smooth.

Pour the mixture into the prepared tin. Arrange the pieces of pear on top and sprinkle with the flaked almonds.

Bake in the oven for 15 minutes, then turn down the oven to 180°C (350°F), Gas mark 4 and cook for a further 10 minutes or until risen and pale golden. The filling should feel firm to the touch in the centre.

Allow to sit in the tin for a few minutes before turning out onto a wire rack. Dust with icing sugar to serve. This is delicious with softly whipped cream.

VARIATIONS

Instead of pears I sometimes use 100g (4oz) raspberries or blackberries (either fresh or frozen) for the topping. Alternatively, I use 50g (2oz) pine nuts instead of fruit. You can also make this with 100g (4oz) peach or nectarine slices, which is particularly nice in the summer!

2 Sweet Celebrations

I adore baking, and love having the excuse to make something sweet. It could be a birthday, anniversary, any other special occasion, or even just for a gossip and a cup of tea with a friend! People always reckon that you are a genius with lots of time on your hands if you have baked something, but really it's often only a matter of getting the oven on, and mixing together a few magic ingredients in a bowl. And what a gorgeous gift it is to make a home-made treat to celebrate someone's special day!

Cardamom Sour-cream Cake

SERVES 6-8 / VEGETARIAN

This is one of the most delicious cakes. It stays wonderfully moist and the flavour of the sour cream or crème fraîche with the cardamom is sublime. This makes a gorgeous birthday cake, or a special gift for Mother's Day.

FOR THE CAKE:
1 egg
200ml tub sour cream or crème fraîche
   (reserve 1 tbsp for icing)
175g (6oz) caster sugar
225g (8oz) plain flour, sifted
$\frac{1}{2}$ tsp bicarbonate of soda
Pinch of salt
1 tsp ground cardamom seeds

FOR THE ICING:
125g (4$\frac{1}{2}$oz) icing sugar, sifted
1 tbsp sour cream or crème fraîche

Preheat the oven to 180°C (350°F), Gas mark 4. Grease the sides of a 20cm (8in) round cake tin and dust with flour; line the base of the tin with a disc of greaseproof paper.

Whisk the egg in a large bowl. Add all but 1 generous tablespoon of the sour cream or crème fraîche and the sugar and whisk to combine. Add the sifted flour and bicarbonate of soda, then the salt and the ground cardamom. Fold the mixture to combine, do not over-mix. Transfer into the tin and place in the oven. Cook for about 35 minutes until the top of the cake just feels firm to the touch and a skewer inserted into the centre comes out clean. Remove from the oven and let it sit for 10 minutes before removing from the tin and cooling on a wire rack.

When the cake has just cooled, make the icing by mixing the reserved tablespoon of sour cream or crème fraîche with the icing sugar. If it is too stiff add just a drop of water. Spread the icing over the top of the cake, allowing any extra icing to drip down the sides.

VARIATION

CARDAMOM SOUR-CREAM BUNS

This recipe works perfectly when cooked in bun cases. They look so sweet with birthday candles in each one. Just divide the mixture between 12 paper cases in a bun or muffin tray (or use a non-stick 12-bun tray) and cook at the same temperature for 18–20 minutes. Ice as above.

Chocolate Cake for Birthday Parties

SERVES 8 / VEGETARIAN

I often make this for my children's birthday parties. One year my youngest requested a cake in the shape of a boy (well, Bob the Builder actually), and I did not have the cake tin required. So, I multiplied this recipe by three and cooked it in two roasting trays (each measuring 30 x 26cm (12 x 10in)). When the cake was cooked, it took every bit of artistic talent that I had to cut it into something that slightly resembled our friend Bob. At least the guests at the party were only three years' old, and had great imaginations!

FOR THE CAKE:
100g (4oz) butter, softened
350g (12oz) caster sugar
2 eggs
225g (8oz) plain flour
50g (2oz) cocoa powder
1 tsp baking powder
1/4 tsp bicarbonate of soda

250ml (8fl oz) buttermilk or sour milk
1 tsp vanilla essence or extract
FOR THE ICING:
285g (10 1/2 oz) icing sugar
2 tsp cocoa powder
3 tsp melted butter
A few tbsp boiling water

Preheat the oven to 180°C (350°F), Gas mark 4. Line the bases of two 22cm (8 1/4 in) or three 18cm (7in) cake tins with greaseproof paper, and grease the sides.

Put the softened butter into a large bowl, add the sugar and beat together until light and fluffy; add the eggs one at a time, beating well. Sieve the flour, cocoa, baking powder and bicarbonate of soda into the butter and sugar mixture, then pour in the buttermilk and add the vanilla essence, stirring well to create a smooth cake dough.

Divide between the cake tins and place in the centre of the preheated oven. Bake for 19–25 minutes, until just set in the centre. When cooked, a skewer inserted into the centre should come out clean. Allow to sit in the tins for 5 minutes, then turn out and cool on a wire rack.

Meanwhile, make the icing. Sieve the icing sugar and cocoa powder into a bowl, then beat in the butter and enough boiling (or hot) water to bring it to spreading consistency. It may only take 1 or 2 tablespoons of water.

Sandwich the cakes together with a layer of icing in the middle. To coat the cake in icing, I find it easiest to place it on an upturned plate. Use a small palette knife or a table knife, and dip it into hot water before and during the icing of the cake; I find this helps give a smooth icing with a shiny gloss.

Porter Cake

SERVES 10-12 / VEGETARIAN

This traditional Irish cake uses porter, such as Guinness, Beamish or Murphy's, and is a deliciously rich and moist fruit cake. Make it a few days in advance of the celebratory event (it's perfect for St Patrick's Day) if you like, and it will improve even more!

450g (1lb) plain flour
1 tsp grated or ground nutmeg
1 tsp mixed spice
1 tsp baking powder
Pinch of salt
225g (8oz) butter
225g (8oz) light brown sugar
450g (1lb) sultanas or raisins or a mixture of both
75g (3oz) chopped candied peel
2 eggs
1 x 330ml bottle of porter or stout

Preheat the oven to 180°C (350°F), Gas mark 4. Line the sides and base of a 20cm (8in) high-sided round cake tin (the sides should be about 7cm (2¾in) high) with greaseproof paper.

Sieve the flour, nutmeg, mixed spice, baking powder and salt into a bowl. Rub in the butter, then stir in the sugar, sultanas or raisins and the candied peel.

Whisk the eggs in another bowl, add the porter or stout, then pour into the dry ingredients and mix well. Empty into the prepared tin and bake for about 2 hours in the preheated oven. If it starts to brown too quickly on top, cover it with foil or greaseproof paper after about 1 hour. The cake is cooked when a skewer inserted into the centre comes out clean. Allow it to sit in the tin for about 20 minutes before turning out and cooling on a wire rack.

Orange and Chocolate Chip Celebratory Cupcakes

MAKES 12 / VEGETARIAN

I love the combination of orange and choc chip, but if you just want plain cupcakes omit the zest and replace the juice with an equal quantity of milk. These would be great for a birthday breakfast!

FOR THE CUPCAKES:

2 eggs

150g (5oz) light brown sugar

Finely grated zest and juice of
    two oranges

Milk

100g (4oz) butter, melted

350g (12oz) plain flour, sifted

1 tbsp baking powder

1/4 tsp bicarbonate of soda

1/2 tsp salt

200g (7oz) dark chocolate, roughly
    chopped into chips

FOR THE ICING:

100g (4oz) icing sugar

Juice of 1/2 orange

Preheat the oven to 200°C (400°F), Gas mark 6. Line a muffin tray with 12 paper muffin cases.

Whisk the eggs and add the sugar and grated orange zest. Measure the juice from the oranges and make it up to 175ml (6fl oz) with milk. Whisk the juice, milk and melted butter into the eggs and sugar, then add the sifted flour, baking powder, bicarbonate of soda, salt and the chopped chocolate. Stir to combine but do not over-mix. Spoon the mixture into the muffin cases and bake in the oven for 18–25 minutes until golden on top and the centre is firm to the touch.

When the cupcakes have cooled, make the orange icing. Sift the icing sugar into a bowl and add 1 teaspoon orange juice. Stir and add a little more juice. Beat the mixture until it comes together and add yet another drop of juice to make an icing of spreadable consistency. If you have made it too wet, add a little more sifted icing sugar.

When the icing is made and the buns are cool, take a small table knife and dip it into a cup of boiling water. This will make it easier to spread the icing on the cupcakes and give it a nice glossy shine. Spread the icing (about 1 teaspoon per cupcake) onto each cake, allow the icing to set for a few minutes and then serve. These cakes keep very well for 4–5 days and can also be frozen.

Lemon Biscuits

MAKES ABOUT 25 / VEGETARIAN

These are incredibly simple and gorgeous biscuits. Do make sure that the butter you use is nice and soft. They are very tasty on their own with a cup of tea or with the Lemon and Ginger Pudding (see page 171). The biscuits can be cut into any kind of shape, such as hearts for Valentine's Day, numbers for a birthday party or little holly leaves or Christmas trees during the festive season.

175g (6oz) plain flour
Finely grated zest of 1 lemon
100g (4oz) butter, softened
50g (2oz) caster sugar

Preheat the oven to 180°C (350°F), Gas mark 4. Put the flour and lemon zest into a mixing bowl, rub in the soft butter, add the caster sugar and bring the whole mixture together to form a stiff dough. Do not add any water.

Roll the dough out to a thickness of about 5mm (1/4in) and cut into shapes. Transfer carefully to a baking tray and bake in the oven for 6–10 minutes until they are pale golden. Cool on a wire rack.

RACHEL'S HANDY TIP
I quite often roll out this dough between two sheets of cling film, as I do for pastry. Chill the slightly flattened piece of dough before rolling out and then the butter does not stick to the cling film.

Wholemeal Shortbread Biscuits

MAKES ABOUT 20 / VEGETARIAN

My boys love making these biscuits so they can choose whatever shapes they like. They are great for birthday parties and lunch boxes. They are also good sandwiched together with raspberry jam!

75g (3oz) wholemeal flour
75g (3oz) plain flour
100g (4oz) butter, softened
50g (2oz) caster sugar

Preheat the oven to 180°C (350°F), Gas mark 4. Place all the ingredients in a food processor and whiz until the mixture almost comes together and resembles coarse breadcrumbs. Then tip onto the work surface and bring it together with your hands. If you are not using a food processor, rub the butter into the combined flour and sugar in a bowl and bring together with your hands.

Sprinkle your work surface with a little flour (brown or white) and roll out the dough until it is about 5mm (1/4in) thick (or roll it between two pieces of cling film, as in the note on page 45). Using a biscuit cutter, cut into whatever shapes you like or just simply into squares with a knife. Transfer onto a baking tray (no need to grease or line it) and bake in the oven for 6–10 minutes depending on the size, or until they are pale golden and feel firm on top. Remove carefully and cool on a wire rack.

Little Almond Brittles

MAKES ABOUT 40 / VEGETARIAN

These are divine little petits-fours, great to serve at the end of a special celebratory meal with coffee. They also make a lovely gift when placed in a small see-through bag and tied with a ribbon.

125g (4¹/₂oz) flaked almonds
225g (8oz) caster sugar
100ml (3¹/₂fl oz) water
75g (3oz) butter
125g (4¹/₂oz) good-quality dark chocolate with at least 70% cocoa solids

Preheat the oven to 180°C (350°F), Gas mark 4. Line two trays with greaseproof paper or non-stick paper.

Place the almonds on a baking tray and toast in the oven for 3-4 minutes until golden – watch them carefully to ensure they don't burn.

Place the sugar, water and butter into a saucepan and stir over a low heat until the sugar has dissolved and the butter melted. Remove the wooden spoon or spatula. Bring to the boil, and boil uncovered for 10–15 minutes or until the mixture is golden brown – watch out as it will be very hot. Do not over-stir this, just swirl the mixture in the pan to prevent it from burning on the bottom. Remove from the heat and add the almonds. Stir to combine, do not over-stir or the mix will turn sugary. Working quickly, place dessertspoonfuls of the mixture on the lined trays and flatten with the back of a wet spoon. Return the pan to the heat for a few seconds if it gets too thick.

Melt the chocolate in a bowl over a pan of simmering water, and drizzle over the brittles (or if you prefer, you can dip the tops of the brittles in the melted chocolate). Allow the chocolate to set, then remove them from the tray and serve or wrap up for gifts. They will keep for a couple of weeks in an airtight container.

Chocolate and Almond Cake with Brandy Cream

SERVES 8 / VEGETARIAN

This is a delicious chocolate cake that uses ground almonds instead of flour, which makes it wonderfully moist. It's an excellent grown-up birthday cake, but if you wish to make this for children, fill it with whipped cream and raspberries instead.

FOR THE CAKE:
125g (4¹/₂oz) dark chocolate
4 eggs
150g (5oz) caster sugar
150g (5oz) ground almonds
Icing sugar, for dusting
FOR THE BRANDY CREAM:
100ml (3¹/₂fl oz) double cream
1–2 tbsp icing sugar
2 tbsp brandy (or another liqueur like rum or Cointreau)

Preheat the oven to 180°C (350°F), Gas mark 4. Prepare two 18cm (7in) cake tins by oiling the sides and lining the bases with discs of greaseproof paper. Melt the chocolate in a bowl by sitting it over a saucepan of gently simmering water.

While the chocolate is melting, place the eggs and sugar in a food mixer and whisk for about 5–8 minutes until light and frothy. When the chocolate has melted, allow to cool for a minute, then pour the egg and sugar mixture gradually onto the chocolate, stirring all the time, and mix until combined. Gently stir in the ground almonds.

Divide the mixture between the two prepared tins and place in the preheated oven. Cook for 17–22 minutes (in my oven they usually take 19 minutes) until the tops of the cakes feel firm in the centre. Allow to cool in the tins for about 10 minutes before carefully transferring to a cooling rack. As they cool, the tops and sides of the cakes will crisp up and crack a little.

Meanwhile make the brandy cream. Whip the cream until just stiff and fold in the sifted icing sugar and brandy. Spread the brandy cream on one cake. Sandwich the cakes together and dust with icing sugar.

Sponge Cake with Rhubarb Cream

SERVES 6-8 / VEGETARIAN

This is a classic Victoria sponge cake, made all the more gorgeous with the rhubarb cream filling. Also try filling it with raspberry jam and whipped cream, sliced strawberries and whipped cream, or with fresh, hand-picked blackberries and cream. This is perfect for Father's or Mother's Day (that's a hint, boys!) or, of course, as a birthday cake.

FOR THE CAKE:
125g (4½oz) butter, softened
175g (6oz) caster sugar
3 eggs
175g (6oz) plain flour
1 tsp baking powder
1 tbsp milk
Icing sugar or caster sugar, for dusting

FOR THE RHUBARB CREAM:
100g (4oz) rhubarb, trimmed and sliced
50g (2oz) sugar
4 tbsp water
75ml (2¾fl oz) double cream

Preheat the oven to 180°C (350°F), Gas mark 4. Grease and flour the sides of two 18cm (7in) cake tins, and line the bases with discs of greaseproof paper.

Cream the butter until soft, then gradually add the sugar, and beat until light and fluffy. Add the eggs one by one, beating well all the time. Sieve the flour and baking powder, and stir in gently, then stir in the milk until just combined.

Divide the mixture between the two tins, hollowing it slightly in the centre, so that it will be flat on top when cooked. Bake for 20–25 minutes, or until the centre of the cake springs back when you push it gently. Turn out onto a wire rack and allow it to cool. (Place the cake that will become the top layer on its base so that the top isn't marked by the cooling rack.)

Meanwhile, place the sliced rhubarb, sugar and water in a saucepan, cover and cook over a gentle heat for about 10 minutes, until the rhubarb is soft. Take off the lid and boil while stirring until it is thick. Pour into a bowl and allow to cool. Whip the cream until it forms soft peaks, then fold in the rhubarb. Sandwich the cakes with the rhubarb cream and sprinkle with sieved icing or caster sugar.

3 Picnics and Days Out

Why is it that food eaten outside just tastes so much better? Even a simple sandwich and a cup of tea tastes like the best meal you have ever had! But something you've made yourself is bound to be a lot more delicious than anything you might buy. I love preparing food to take on a picnic or to the beach, or to bring to the woods for a mid-walk snack (a good incentive to get the children out walking). You might only go as far as your own back garden, it doesn't matter. My children love the novelty of gathering up the picnic blanket, putting food in a basket and finding a nice spot to eat. I'm sure the fresh air makes them eat that bit more too, which is always good!

Muffleta

SERVES 6-8

This is made from a hollowed-out loaf of bread with the top cut off and saved to make the lid. It's filled with layers of different fillings, then pressed for a few hours and cut into wedges so that each slice has a bit of crust surrounding a wonderful layered filling. It looks so impressive, but could not be easier to make. Vary the ingredients according to your taste. It's best if made a day in advance, so it can be pressed overnight in the fridge.

4 **red onions, peeled and cut into wedges**
1 tbsp **olive oil**
Sea salt and freshly ground pepper
1 **round loaf of bread about 20cm (8in) in diameter**
2 tbsp **Basil Pesto (see page 217), mixed with 1 tbsp olive oil**
3 slices **Parma or Serrano ham**

4 **preserved roasted peppers (see page 177)**
250g (9oz) **soft goats' cheese, cut into slices**
1 tbsp **Olive Paste (see page 102), mixed with 1 tbsp olive oil**
6-8 **thin slices of salami**
1 **large handful of rocket leaves**

Preheat the oven to 200°C (400°F), Gas mark 6. Toss the red onion with the olive oil on a baking tray, season and roast in the oven for 10-15 minutes or until soft. Set aside.

Using a serrated bread knife, slice the top off the loaf of bread and set aside until later. Scoop out most of the bread from inside the loaf and put to one side.

Spread the pesto and olive oil around the inside of the loaf and the cut side of the lid. Place half the Parma or Serrano ham in the base of the loaf, if using, then half of the pieces of roast peppers, followed by half the goats' cheese. Then drizzle half the tapenade or olive paste over the cheese, followed by the slices of salami, if using, and then the roasted red onions and lastly the rocket leaves.

Season with sea salt and pepper and repeat with the second half of all the ingredients. You might need to press it down gently with the palms of your hands to fit everything in – it should be very full or it will fall apart when you try to slice it. When you have finished with all the ingredients, place the lid on top.

Wrap the loaf in cling film, put it on a plate then place a side plate or board with weights or even jars of jam or anything heavy on top and place in the fridge. This will weigh it down, which will make it easier to cut into slices. Leave for 3 hours to 1 day, unwrap and cut into wedges to serve.

RACHEL'S HANDY TIP

You can always whiz up the discarded bread to make breadcrumbs for the freezer.

Chest of Sandwiches

MAKES ABOUT 15 SANDWICHES

This was ingeniously created by my husband's grandmother, Myrtle Allen. It's similar to the muffleta on the previous page, but for this you open the top of a loaf of bread like a flap, cut out the inside, make little sandwiches out of what you've taken out and miraculously pop them all back into the hollow 'chest'. What could be better to take on a long walk or to the races? Talk about picnic envy!

900g (2lb) rectangular loaf of unsliced bread
Sandwich fillings, such as Cheddar cheese and chutney (see pages 178–81);
  cooked chicken mixed with Mayonnaise (see page 216); smoked salmon
  and Cucumber Pickle (see page 174)

Insert a bread knife into one long side of the loaf, just above the bottom crust. Push the knife through until it reaches, but does not go through, the crust on the far side. Without making the cut through which the knife was inserted any bigger, work the knife in a fan shape from side to side, then pull it out. The bread should now be cut away from the bottom crust inside but without a very noticeable mark on the exterior of the loaf. This takes some practice, so you may wish to have an extra loaf spare the first time.

Next, cut through the top of the loaf to make a lid, carefully leaving one long side uncut as a hinge. When you open it, if it looks in danger of falling off, keep it propped up from behind with a couple of jars or something similar.

Finally, with the lid open, cut the bread away from the sides just inside of the crust on all sides and down to 1cm (½in) of the bottom crust. Ease the bread out carefully – it should turn out in a solid brick, leaving an empty case behind.

Cut the brick into four long, horizontal slices (cut it in half lengthways first to make it easier if you like) and make two long sandwiches using the fillings of your choice. Cut each big sandwich into four or five small finger sandwiches, press them together firmly and put them back into the chest. Surprise your friends by presenting the loaf and letting them open it up to find the treasure inside!

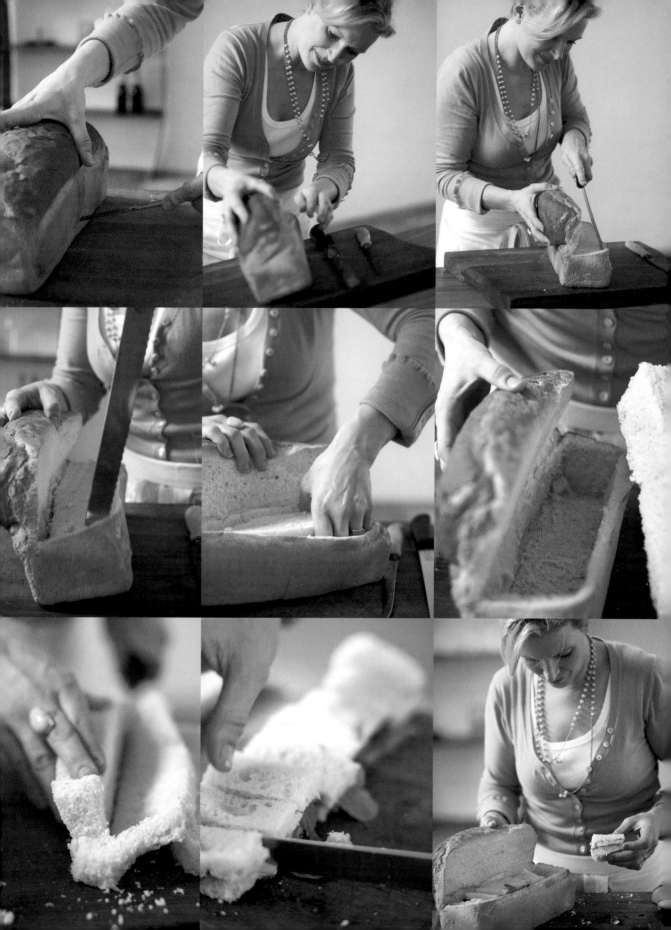

Salad of Haricot Beans with Tomatoes and Tuna

SERVES 3-4 / VEGETARIAN

This is one of those great salads that can be put together in no time. It's fresh and delicious and is made from ingredients that you're likely to have in your kitchen at any time.

FOR THE DRESSING:
3 tbsp olive oil
2 tbsp lemon juice
Salt and freshly ground black pepper

FOR THE SALAD:
1 x 410g tin of cooked haricot beans, drained

1 x 200g tin of tuna, drained and broken into chunks
150g (5oz) cherry tomatoes, quartered
2 spring onions, trimmed and thinly sliced
1-2 tbsp chopped fresh marjoram or mint

In a small jug, mix together the olive oil, lemon juice and seasoning. Assemble the remaining ingredients in a bowl and then drizzle over the dressing and toss.

Rocket, Tomato and Sugar Snap Pea Salad

SERVES 4-6 / VEGETARIAN

This is also a lovely fresh, light summer salad.

FOR THE DRESSING:
2 tbsp olive oil
1 tbsp lemon juice or cider vinegar
½ tsp wholegrain mustard
Pinch of sugar
Salt and freshly ground black pepper

FOR THE SALAD:
175g (6oz) sugar snap peas, topped and tailed
150g (5oz) rocket
250g (9oz) cherry tomatoes, halved or quartered

Whisk the dressing ingredients together and season to taste. Bring a pan of salted water up to the boil and add the peas. Boil for 2-3 minutes, until they still have a bit of bite, then drain and refresh in cold water and pat dry. Mix the peas, rocket and cherry tomatoes in a bowl. Drizzle the dressing over the salad and toss.

Duck, Lentil and Red Cabbage Salad
SERVES 4-6

This is a really delicious and very portable salad, and can also be prepared in advance. Leftover roast chicken works well as a substitute for the duck breast.

200g (7oz) duck breast
Salt and freshly ground black pepper
50g (2oz) roasted hazelnuts
200g (7oz) lentils
4 tbsp olive oil
Juice of 1 lemon
1/2-1 red chilli, deseeded and finely chopped
1/4 red cabbage, about 300g (11oz), core removed and very thinly sliced
3 tbsp chopped fresh coriander

Preheat the oven to 200°C (400°F), Gas mark 6. Using the tip of a knife, make three or four shallow incisions through the skin of the duck breast. Season the fat side with salt and pepper and drizzle with a tiny bit of olive oil. Place fat-side-down in an unheated frying pan or grill pan. Turn the heat on low and cook the duck breast very slowly, until golden brown, allowing the fat to render out – this may take 15-20 minutes. Turn the duck breast over and continue to cook for another 5-10 minutes, until it is just cooked through, or pop it into the oven on a roasting tray for the final 5-10 minutes.

Meanwhile, roast the hazelnuts by tossing them in a dry frying pan over a medium heat until golden, or put them into the oven with the duck for 5-7 minutes - but on a separate roasting tray.

While the duck is cooking, put the lentils in a saucepan and cover with cold water, bring up to the boil and cook for 15-20 minutes until soft. Drain and toss with the olive oil, lemon juice and chopped chilli and season to taste. Add the sliced red cabbage and chopped coriander and stir to mix. Taste and add a little more olive oil if it is a bit dry or more lemon juice if it needs sharpening up.

When the duck is cooked and has cooled slightly, slice it very thinly and toss with the salad. Tip into a large bowl or pile onto salad plates and sprinkle with the chopped roasted hazelnuts.

Asparagus and Spring Onion Tart

SERVES 6-8 / VEGETARIAN

This is one of the very best savoury tarts and it is perfect in the late spring/early summer when asparagus is in season. It is light and delicate in flavour, and has a wonderful crisp shortcrust pastry base.

25cm (10in) Shortcrust Pastry case, baked blind (see page 220)
1 tbsp olive oil
200g (7oz) spring onions, trimmed and finely sliced or chopped
200g (7oz) asparagus spears, trimmed
Salt and freshly ground black pepper
4 eggs
350ml (12fl oz) double cream
25g (1oz) Parmesan cheese, finely grated

Preheat the oven to 180°C (350°F), Gas mark 4. To make the tart filling, heat the olive oil in a small saucepan, add the spring onions and cook over a low heat until soft. Cook the asparagus by dropping it into boiling water with a pinch of salt, cover and bring back up to the boil, then remove the lid and boil, uncovered, for 3-4 minutes until it is just cooked. Drain, and then slice the asparagus into lengths 3cm (1½in) long, at an angle.

Whisk the eggs in a bowl, add the cream and the cooked spring onions and season. Pour this filling into the cooked pastry shell, still in the tin. Drop the asparagus into the tart and sprinkle the grated Parmesan cheese over the top. Carefully place the tart into the preheated oven and cook for 20-30 minutes, or until the tart is just set in the centre. Remove from the oven, and serve out of the tin, hot or at room temperature.

Potato, Chorizo and Feta Frittata

SERVES 8

A frittata is the best thing to eat outdoors and is just as fantastic hot or cold. For a vegetarian option you can leave out the chorizo.

250g (9oz) potatoes, peeled and cubed into 1cm (½in) pieces
6 tbsp olive oil
1 onion, peeled and sliced
8 eggs
100ml (3½fl oz) single cream

1 tsp salt
1 tbsp chopped fresh marjoram
125g (4½oz) chorizo, sliced
125g (4½oz) feta cheese, crumbled

Preheat the oven to 180°C (350°F), Gas mark 4. Place the potatoes in a saucepan, cover with boiling water and boil for 5 minutes, or until just cooked. Do not over-cook or they will go mushy. Drain and set aside.

Heat a 25cm (10in) ovenproof frying pan, add 3 tablespoons of olive oil and the sliced onion, cover with a saucepan lid and sweat over a gentle heat until soft and slightly golden. Set aside.

Whisk the eggs in a bowl, add the cream, 1 teaspoon salt and the marjoram. Stir in the sliced chorizo, the cooked onions and potatoes.

Heat 3 tablespoons of olive oil in the frying pan. When it is hot, pour in the egg mixture and stir briefly to distribute the ingredients evenly. Top with the crumbled feta cheese. Place in the preheated oven and bake for 25–35 minutes or until set in the centre. Remove from the oven and allow to cool a little before sliding it onto a large serving plate or a large cake tin lined with baking parchment, if you want to transport it on a picnic. Serve warm or at room temperature.

VARIATION

BUTTERNUT SQUASH, CHORIZO AND FETA FRITTATA
Follow the recipe above but replace the potato with the same weight of butternut squash, peeled (with a knife), deseeded and cubed.

Ham and Egg Pie

SERVES 6-8

This is such a lovely, old-fashioned picnic pie.

200g (7oz) Shortcrust Pastry, made with 125g (4¹/₂oz) flour,
   75g (3oz) butter, pinch of salt and ¹/₂-1 egg, following
   the instructions on page 220

FOR THE FILLING:

15g (¹/₂oz) butter
1 onion, peeled and chopped
6 eggs
75ml (2³/₄fl oz) double cream
150g (5oz) cooked ham or cooked bacon rashers,
   sliced into 1 x 2cm (¹/₂ x 3/₄in) pieces
1 tbsp chopped parsley
Salt and freshly ground black pepper

Preheat the oven to 180°C (350°F), Gas mark 4. Roll out the pastry and line a 25cm (10in) ovenproof plate. Trim the pastry so that it is a bit bigger than the plate, and then fold up the edges slightly so that you have a slight lip all the way around. This will prevent the cream from running off the plate when you put it in the oven. Place the pastry on its plate in the fridge while you prepare the filling ingredients.

For the filling, melt the butter in a small saucepan, add the onions and cook over a gentle heat until soft. Whisk two of the eggs in a bowl, add the cream, the cooked onions, chopped ham and parsley. Season with salt and pepper to taste. Pour this into the pastry case. Carefully break the remaining eggs onto the tart, trying to keep the egg yolks intact.

Bake for 25–35 minutes in the preheated oven until the custard is set in the centre and the eggs on top are just cooked. Serve warm or allow to cool and pack for a picnic. Cut slices of the tart straight from the plate.

Maple Syrup and Pecan Muffins

MAKES 12 / VEGETARIAN

These are gorgeous muffins and are great for a picnic or children's lunch boxes.
They will keep for 4–5 days and also freeze well.

FOR THE MUFFINS:
1 egg
50g (2oz) oats
75ml (2³/₄fl oz) maple syrup
225ml (7¹/₂fl oz) milk
75g (3oz) butter, softened not melted
75g (3oz) light brown sugar
225g (8oz) plain flour, sifted
3 tsp baking powder
¹/₂ tsp salt
75g (3oz) chopped pecans or walnuts

FOR THE GLAZE (OPTIONAL):
50g (2oz) butter, softened
50g (2oz) icing sugar, sifted
1 tbsp maple syrup
12 pecans

Preheat the oven to 200°C (400°F), Gas mark 6. Line a muffin tray with
12 paper muffin cases.

Whisk the egg in a bowl, add the oats, maple syrup and milk and whisk to
combine. Set aside to soak while you prepare the other ingredients.

In a large bowl beat the butter, add the sugar, and mix to make a soft paste.
Gradually add the milk mixture, stirring all the time, then stir in the sifted flour,
baking powder, salt and chopped nuts, until just combined. Do not over-stir.

Spoon the mixture into the paper cases in the tin and bake in the preheated
oven for 18–25 minutes until the tops are golden and feel firm to the touch in
the centre. Take out of the tin and allow to cool on a wire rack.

Make the glaze, if using, by mixing together the butter, sugar and syrup.
Using a knife, spread the glaze over the tops of the cooled muffins and top
each muffin with a pecan.

Jam Tarts
MAKES 12 / VEGETARIAN

These are a great way to use up leftover sweet or savoury pastry; my children love making them for our picnics. There are few things more delicious on a picnic than a jam tart with a cup of tea, so don't forget to bring some in a flask!

150g (5oz) Sweet or Savoury Shortcrust Pastry (see page 220)
12 tsp summer fruit, apricot, raspberry or strawberry jam

Preheat the oven to 200°C (400°F), Gas mark 6. Roll out the pastry between two sheets of cling film to a thickness of about 3mm (1/8in). Using a 6cm (2½in) cutter, cut out 12 rounds (you may need to gather up the scraps and re-roll the pastry).

Press the rounds into a shallow patty tin (you can use paper cases if you wish) and drop a teaspoon of jam into each. Cook in the preheated oven for 8–12 minutes until the pastry is golden and the jam bubbling. Allow to cool slightly in the tin before carefully transferring to a wire rack (the jam will thicken as it cools).

4 Food for Children

People often ask me what I cook for my children and how I get them to eat good nutritious food. Well, in this chapter I have included many of my boys' favourite things to eat so that you can see for yourself there is no trick – it just tastes good! This is simple, foolproof, no-fuss food that is easy to prepare, which makes it ideal if your children want to help you in the kitchen. I have included great ideas for breakfast, lunch, supper and for yummy snacks as well.

Yoghurt with Oats and Honey

SERVES 1 / VEGETARIAN

This is more a simple combination than a recipe, and is a fantastic, healthy, and very quick breakfast. The oats, with their slow-releasing carbohydrates, will keep your little ones going until lunch. Add some fruit too, if you wish, such as raspberries, blueberries, sliced strawberries, peaches or pears.

4-6 tbsp really good yoghurt, natural or with fruit
1 small handful of porridge oats
1 tsp honey

Place the yoghurt in a bowl, sprinkle with oats, drizzle with honey and serve.

Scrambled Eggs on Toast

SERVES 2 / VEGETARIAN

There is nothing like a classic scrambled egg on toast for breakfast or brunch, or even supper! Made in about two minutes, it's a perfect quick meal for hungry kids.

3 free-range eggs, best quality possible
2 tbsp milk (a little single cream mixed with the milk is, of course, divine!)
Salt and freshly ground black pepper
2 slices wholemeal bread
15g (½oz butter)

Break the eggs into a bowl, add the milk and seasoning, and whisk for about 10 seconds. Pop the slices of bread in the toaster. Put the butter into a cold saucepan, add the egg mixture and stir continuously with a wooden spoon over a low heat until the mixture looks scrambled but still soft and creamy. Check the seasoning and serve, piled onto buttered toast.

Super Smoothies

EACH SERVES 4-6 / VEGETARIAN

Smoothies are a great way to get little ones to have some fruit, and my children love these combinations in particular. The Nectarine, Berry and Plum Smoothie has oats in it, which will keep children's energy topped up for a few hours as the oats contain slow-releasing carbohydrates. It's good for their concentration levels, too.

BANANA AND CINNAMON SMOOTHIE
4 bananas
500ml (18fl oz) natural yoghurt
2-4 tsp honey
1 tsp ground cinnamon

Whiz all the ingredients together in a blender or food processor and serve.

NECTARINE, BERRY AND PLUM SMOOTHIE
2 nectarines, stones removed
2 tbsp raspberries, blueberries or blackberries
2 plums, stones removed
400ml (14fl oz) natural yoghurt
2 tbsp oats
Juice of 1/2 lemon
1 tbsp honey
10 ice cubes (optional)

Whiz all the ingredients together in a blender or food processor, adding more honey or lemon juice if you prefer a sweeter or sharper flavour respectively.

Quesadillas

MAKES 8 WEDGES / VEGETARIAN

Quesadillas are essentially the Central American toasted cheese sandwich! We make many versions of it at home, depending on what is in the fridge. Our children love plain cheese quesadillas or quesadillas filled with chicken or a little spinach (very handy as you can sneak it in almost unnoticed to greens-wary little ones). These are perfect for a snack or TV supper, and they are great for grown-ups too. I quite often have guacamole and tomato salsa with mine, as they do in Mexico, or else for a very fast sauce try Crème Fraîche with Sweet Chilli (see page 139). Not all children like chilli, but one of our boys actually likes it, so I sometimes leave it in for him.

2 wheat flour tortillas
100g (4oz) cheese (I like a mixture of Cheddar,
    Gruyère and mozzarella), grated
1 spring onion, trimmed and sliced (optional)
½ green or red chilli, deseeded and chopped finely
    (optional – chillies can be very hot!)

Heat a frying pan slightly. Place one tortilla in the pan and sprinkle with all the grated cheese, the sliced spring onion and chilli, if using. Cover with the other tortilla and press down with a spatula or your hands. The cheese will have started melting at this stage and the tortilla on the bottom should be golden brown. When it is, carefully turn it over and then cook the other side for another couple of minutes, until it is golden and all the cheese has melted. Transfer to a board and cut into wedges. Serve immediately on its own or with Crème Fraîche with Sweet Chilli or Tomato and Cucumber Salsa (see page 139).

VARIATIONS

QUESADILLAS WITH CHICKEN
Make as for the basic quesadillas, but add 75g (3oz) shredded cooked chicken with the grated cheese.

QUESADILLAS WITH SPINACH
Make as for the basic quesadillas, but add one handful of baby spinach leaves (about 15g (½oz)) with the grated cheese.

Parmesan Chicken Goujons

SERVES 6-8

These are one of my boys' favourite foods. Use good-quality free-range chicken and you'll have a delicious and nutritious meal that little ones will adore. My children love dipping these goujons into homemade Tomato Ketchup (see page 80) or Mayonnaise (see page 216), or sometimes a mixture of the two!

600g (1lb 6oz) boneless and skinless
   chicken
50g (2oz) plain flour
Salt and freshly ground black pepper
2 eggs, beaten

100g (4oz) breadcrumbs
50g (2oz) Parmesan cheese,
   or something similar, such as
   Grana Padano, finely grated
3 tbsp sunflower oil

These can either be cooked on the hob or in the oven. If using the oven, preheat to 200°C (400°F), Gas mark 6 and place a baking tray in the oven to preheat.

Cut the chicken into goujons the size of a big finger (1 x 10cm (1/2 x 4in)). Place the flour in a mixing bowl or in a plastic bag with some salt and pepper. Place the beaten eggs in another bowl. Mix the breadcrumbs and finely grated cheese together and place in a bowl or bag as well.

Toss the goujons in the seasoned flour, making sure they do not stick together, then remove. Shake off the excess flour and dip them in the beaten egg. Remove from the egg, letting the excess drip off, and toss into the breadcrumb and cheese mix. Shake off the excess and lay the goujons on a plate.

To cook on the hob, heat the oil in a large frying pan over a medium to high heat. When the oil is hot, add the goujons in a single layer, cook on one side for about 3 minutes until golden, then turn down the heat and flip the pieces over. Cook on the other side for about 4 minutes, until cooked through and golden.

To cook the goujons in the oven, drizzle the base of the preheated baking tray with the oil and lay the floured and seasoned goujons in a single layer. Bake in the oven for about 12–18 minutes, turning the goujons over halfway through, or when golden on one side. When they are completely cooked, remove from the oven and serve.

PARMESAN FISH GOUJONS

Also known as fish fingers! Prepare as for chicken, but substitute skinned and filleted fish. Cut into finger size goujons as before. For this recipe I use firm fish, such as cod, hake or ling. Cooking time remains the same.

Tomato Ketchup

MAKES 400ML (14FL OZ) / VEGETARIAN

If your children regularly eat ketchup, then you might want to give them something a bit healthier and more delicious, like this real tomato ketchup. If you think they won't like this version, ease them into it by mixing some into their usual type and gradually adjust their taste. This is definitely best made in the summer with ripe red tomatoes.

2 tbsp olive oil
225g (8oz) onions, peeled and
    roughly chopped
600g (1lb 6oz) tomatoes, roughly
    chopped (no need to peel)
2 garlic cloves, peeled and crushed
75ml (2³/₄fl oz) white wine vinegar

75g (3oz) sugar
2 tsp Dijon mustard
¹/₂ tsp ground allspice
¹/₂ tsp ground cloves
¹/₂ tsp salt
¹/₂ tsp freshly ground black pepper

Heat the olive oil in a saucepan, add the onions and toss over a medium heat until cooked and a little golden. Add the rest of the ingredients and simmer with the lid on for about 30 minutes, until very soft.

Remove from the heat and whiz in a liquidiser or food processor. Pour through a sieve into a clean saucepan and simmer, uncovered and stirring regularly, for another 30 minutes, or until the mixture is thick.

Pour into sterilised jars or bottles (see page 177) and cover with lids.

Classic Spaghetti and Meatballs with Fresh Tomato Sauce

SERVES 6 (OR ABOUT 10 CHILDREN)

We used to have meatballs when we were little, and now our boys love them too. Children just love slurping up the spaghetti!

FOR THE MEATBALLS:
2 tbsp olive oil
1 onion, peeled and finely chopped
1 garlic clove, peeled and crushed
900g (2lb) freshly minced beef
2 tbsp chopped fresh herbs, such as marjoram, or a smaller quantity of rosemary
1 egg, beaten
Salt and freshly ground black pepper

FOR THE TOMATO SAUCE:
3 tbsp olive oil
100g (4oz) onion, peeled and sliced
1 garlic clove, peeled and crushed
2 x 410g tins chopped tomatoes (or use 900g (2lb) ripe, peeled (see page 178) and chopped tomatoes)
Salt, sugar and freshly ground black pepper

TO SERVE:
3 tbsp olive oil
150g (5oz) mozzarella, grated
450g (1lb) spaghetti

To make the meatballs, heat the olive oil in a heavy, stainless-steel saucepan over a gentle heat and add the onion and garlic. Cover and sweat for 4 minutes, until soft and a little golden, then allow to cool.

In a bowl, mix the minced beef with the cold sweated onion and garlic, then add the herbs and the beaten egg. Season the mixture to taste. Fry a tiny bit to check the seasoning and adjust if necessary. Divide the mixture into about 24 round balls and place in a dish. Cover the meatballs and refrigerate until required.

Meanwhile, make the tomato sauce. Heat the oil in a stainless-steel saucepan. Add the sliced onion and crushed garlic, toss until coated, cover and sweat over a gentle heat until soft and a tiny bit golden. Add the tomatoes, mix and season with salt, freshly ground pepper and a pinch of sugar. Gently simmer, uncovered, for approximately 30 minutes or until softened.

Heat up a frying pan over a medium heat with about 3 tablespoons of olive oil. Cook the meatballs for about 10 minutes. When they are done, transfer into a dish, add the tomato sauce and sprinkle the grated cheese on top. Place under a preheated grill to let the cheese melt.

Meanwhile, cook the spaghetti in a pan of boiling water. Drain and serve on individual plates with the meatballs piled on top.

Party Sausages with Mustard and Honey Dip
SERVES 10-12

This is really fast and easy and can be served with the Homemade Pork Sausages on page 196, or with store-bought cocktail sausages if you are in a hurry and have a lot of little mouths to feed. The dip is slightly sweet from the honey, which works very well with the sausages. The Dijon mustard is not very hot, although you can add more mustard if you prefer and are serving to adults.

FOR THE SAUSAGES:
1 quantity of Homemade Pork
   Sausages (see page 196) or 40
   cocktail sausages

FOR THE DIP:
250ml (8fl oz) crème fraîche
1 tbsp grainy mustard
1/2 tsp honey
1 tsp Dijon mustard

Cook the sausages in a frying pan, under the grill or in a hot oven.

In a serving bowl, mix together all of the dip ingredients to combine. When the sausages are cooked, place the bowl of dip in the centre of a large serving plate and arrange the sausages around.

Banana and Peanut Butter Muffins

MAKES 12 / VEGETARIAN

We all adore these muffins at home; they are sweet, delicious and nutty. They are also great for a snack or to take on a picnic. Put them in your kids' lunch boxes for a nice surprise!

275g (10oz) plain flour
50g (2oz) oats
1 tbsp baking power
2 eggs
150g (5oz) light brown sugar
2 bananas (200g (7oz)), peeled and mashed
125g (4¹/₂oz) crunchy peanut butter
50g (2oz) butter, melted
250ml (8fl oz) milk

Preheat the oven to 190°C (375°F), Gas mark 5. Line a muffin pan with 12 paper muffin cases.

Place the flour, oats and baking powder in a bowl, mix together and set aside. In another bowl, whisk the eggs, add the light brown sugar, mashed bananas, peanut butter and the melted butter. Stir to mix, then add the milk and stir to combine. Add the dry ingredients and fold in gently, do not over-mix.

Spoon the mixture into the prepared muffin cases and bake for 18–24 minutes, or until the tops spring back when gently touched. Allow to stand in the muffin pan for a minute before turning out to cool on a wire rack.

Drop Scones

MAKES 12 / VEGETARIAN

These little drop scones (or crumpets) are quite delicious and are very easy to make. They are fabulous for brunch or for a quick snack in the afternoon. My children love making these after school when they are always a bit peckish.

100g (4oz) self-raising flour
1 tsp baking powder
25g (1oz) caster sugar
Pinch of salt
1 egg
125ml (4fl oz) milk
Drop of sunflower oil, for greasing

Sift the flour and baking powder into a bowl, add the sugar and salt and stir to mix. Make a well in the centre, crack in the egg and whisk, gradually drawing in the flour from the edge. Add the milk gradually, whisking all the time, to form a smooth batter.

Lightly grease a frying pan and warm it over a moderate heat. Drop 3 tablespoons of the batter into the pan, keeping them well apart so they do not stick together. Cook for about 2 minutes or until bubbles appear on the surface and begin to burst and the drop scones are golden underneath, then flip them over and cook on the other side for a minute or until golden on this side as well.

Remove from the pan and serve warm with butter and jam, apple jelly, Lemon Curd (see page 186) or, if you are like my children, chocolate spread! (If you wish, wrap the drop scones in a clean tea towel to keep warm while you make the rest.)

Chewy Seedy Oat and Apricot Bars

MAKES ABOUT 18 BARS / VEGETARIAN

Pack these in lunch boxes, but always be sure to steal one for yourself to enjoy with a cup of coffee once the kids have gone to school!

300g (11oz) porridge oats
100g (4oz) pumpkin or sunflower
    seeds, or a mixture of the two
50g (2oz) desiccated coconut
50g (2oz) plain flour
200g (7oz) butter

200g (7oz) golden syrup
150g (5oz) soft brown sugar
150g (5oz) dried apricots, chopped
125g (4¹/₂oz) crunchy peanut butter
1 tsp vanilla extract

Preheat the oven to 160°C (325°F), Gas mark 3. Line an 18 x 28cm (7 x 11in) Swiss roll tin with non-stick baking parchment, leaving a little hanging over the edges for easy removal later.

Place the oats, seeds, coconut and flour in a large bowl and mix together. Melt the butter and golden syrup together in a saucepan, then mix in the sugar, chopped apricots, peanut butter and vanilla extract. Pour into the bowl of dry ingredients and mix until evenly combined.

Press the mixture into the prepared tin and bake in the oven for 20–25 minutes, or until golden and slightly firm. Allow to cool in the tin, then remove, still in the paper, and cut into 18 bars (or cut them depending on whatever size you want them to be). Store in an air-tight container for up to 1 week. These will also freeze well.

White Soda Scones

MAKES ABOUT 12 SCONES / VEGETARIAN

This has to be one of the fastest and most delicious scones you can make. The dough is just perfect for children to play around with, even if it does then get heavy from over-handling. You should see some of the creations that my sons make; dinosaurs are their favourites! This is the soda bread mixture we make at the Ballymaloe Cookery School, and there are countless variations you can experiment with from this basic recipe.

450g (1lb) plain white flour
1 tsp salt

1 tsp bicarbonate of soda
400ml (14fl oz) buttermilk or sour milk

Preheat the oven to 230°C (450°F), Gas mark 8. Sift the flour, salt and bicarbonate of soda into a large bowl, and rub the mixture in with your fingertips to incorporate some air. Make a well in the centre and pour in most of the buttermilk. Using one hand, with your fingers open and stiff, mix in a full circle, bringing the flour and liquid together, adding more liquid if necessary. The dough should be quite soft, but not too sticky.

Turn it out onto a floured surface, and do not knead it but gently bring it into one ball. Flatten it slightly to a height of about 3cm (1½in). Cut the dough into squares or whatever shape you like. Put the scones onto a baking tray and pop into the hot oven and cook for 10–15 minutes (depending on the size). Have a look at them after 10 minutes; if they are deep golden brown, then turn down the heat to 200°C (400°F), Gas mark 6 for the remainder of the time. When cooked they should sound hollow when tapped. Cool on a wire rack.

VARIATIONS

HERB SCONES
Add 1–2 tbsp of chopped thyme, rosemary, parsley, chives, marjoram, savoury or sage to the flour before you pour in the buttermilk. For even more flavour, you could sprinkle the tops with grated Cheddar cheese before they go into the oven.

PESTO SCONES
Add 1–2 tbsp basil pesto to the buttermilk before mixing with the flour. These are also delicious with chopped olives mixed in with the flour.

CRISPY BACON AND PARMESAN SCONES

Add about 75g (3oz) crispy bacon, a good pinch of cayenne pepper and 50g (2oz) finely grated Parmesan cheese to the flour at the start, then brush the tops of the raw scones with beaten egg or leftover buttermilk and sprinkle with more grated Parmesan cheese.

SWEET SCONES

Add 25g (1oz) caster sugar to the dry ingredients. Also, put 1 egg into a measuring jug, lightly beat and make up to 400ml (14fl oz) with the buttermilk or sour milk. This makes the dough slightly richer. In addition, you could add any of the following ingredients to the flour at the start of the recipe: 100g (4oz) sultanas (or raisins or currants) and 1/2 teaspoon mixed spice; 100g (4oz) chopped chocolate; or 1 teaspoon ground cinnamon and an extra 25g (1oz) sugar. Then brush the tops with beaten egg and dip into 50g (2oz) granulated sugar mixed with 1/2 teaspoon ground cinnamon.

Jam Drops

MAKES ABOUT 30 / VEGETARIAN

These are quick little biscuits which makes them great to prepare with children since they won't lose their concentration halfway through. My boys love baking them!

200g (7oz) self-raising flour
100g (4oz) caster sugar
100g (4oz) slightly soft butter

1 small egg, beaten
Strawberry, raspberry or apricot jam

Preheat the oven to 190°C (375°F), Gas mark 5. In a food processor mix the self-raising flour, caster sugar and butter together. Add just enough egg to bring the mixture together to form a stiff dough. If you are not using a food processor, rub the butter into the flour and sugar, then add enough egg and with your hands work it until it forms a stiff dough.

Roll the mixture into balls the size of a walnut and place on a baking tray (no need to line). Flatten each ball slightly and make a small indentation in the middle of each biscuit with your thumb or the end of a wooden spoon. Drop half a teaspoon of jam in the centre. Bake for 10–15 minutes until just golden. Cool on a wire rack.

5 Extended Family

My extended family not only includes relatives (grandparents, in-laws, aunts, uncles and cousins), it also includes those close friends and neighbours we know so well that they may as well be family! The food in this chapter is for all those easy, casual occasions when the whole gang gets together.

Winter Vegetable Broth with Haricot Beans and Chorizo

SERVES 6

This soup is the best thing in winter time – comforting and nutritious. It's a meal in itself for lunch. And, even better, it's very easy to make.

2 tbsp olive oil
1 onion, peeled and chopped
1 large carrot, peeled and chopped
2 small leaks, trimmed and chopped
2 potatoes, peeled and chopped
2 large garlic cloves, peeled and crushed

150g (5oz) chorizo, sliced about 3mm (1/8in) thick
900ml (1½ pints) chicken stock
1 x 410g tin haricot beans, drained
2 tbsp chopped fresh coriander or parsley
Salt and freshly ground black pepper

Heat the olive oil in a large saucepan. Add the onion, carrot, leeks, potatoes, garlic and chorizo. Cover and sweat for 10 minutes over a low heat, stirring every now and then.

Add the chicken stock and drained haricot beans. Bring to the boil and simmer for 5 minutes until all the vegetables are cooked. Add the herbs, season to taste and serve.

Light Coconut Broth with Pak Choi and Basil

SERVES 8

I absolutely love this kind of recipe; you throw a few things in a pot, boil for a few minutes and end up with the most delicious result. I also adore these South-east Asian flavours.

2.4 litres (4 pints) vegetable (or light chicken) stock
2 x 410g tins coconut milk
2 red chillies, deseeded and finely sliced into rings
4 spring onions, trimmed and sliced thinly at an angle
2 garlic cloves, peeled and crushed
2 heaped tsp grated ginger
4 heads pak choi, stalk and leaves shredded
6 tbsp Thai fish sauce (nam pla)
Juice of 1 lime
4 tbsp sliced basil

Place the stock, coconut milk, chilli, spring onions, garlic and ginger in a saucepan and bring up to the boil. Add the pak choi and continue cooking for 1–2 minutes or until the pak choi is just cooked. Add the fish sauce, lime juice and basil. You probably won't need any additional salt since the fish sauce is already quite salty. Serve in warm bowls.

VARIATION
LIGHT COCONUT BROTH WITH PAK CHOI AND PRAWNS
Add 32 peeled tiger or or other large prawns into the broth with the shredded pak choi and cook as above. The prawns will cook in the same time as the pak choi.

Asparagus with Easy Hollandaise Sauce

SERVES 4 AS A MAIN COURSE OR 8 AS A STARTER / VEGETARIAN

I love it when the first asparagus appears in the shops in late spring. These bright green spears are so delicious cooked simply in a little salted boiling water. There are few things much better than a big feast of asparagus and a divine bowl of homemade hollandaise sauce, mopped up with toasted bread and washed down with a glass of wine!

32 spears fresh green asparagus
4-8 slices good-quality white bread
Soft butter, for the toast
FOR THE HOLLANDAISE SAUCE:
2 egg yolks
100g (4oz) butter, cubed
1-2 tsp lemon juice

To make the hollandaise sauce, place the egg yolks in a heatproof glass bowl. Heat the butter in a saucepan until foaming, then pour gradually onto the egg yolks, whisking all the time. Add the lemon juice to taste, then pour into a heatproof measuring jug. Half-fill a saucepan with hot water from the kettle and place the jug of hollandaise in the saucepan to keep warm. When the water cools, just put the saucepan on a gentle heat, but do not let the water boil too long or the sauce will scramble.

Keep the sauce warm while you are waiting to serve it; it will sit quite happily like this for a couple of hours.

Half-fill a saucepan with water, add a good pinch of salt and bring to the boil. While it is heating up, remove the woody ends from the asparagus spears by snapping off about 3-4cm (1¼-1½in) of the bottom of the stalk. Discard the woody ends.

Cook the asparagus by dropping it into the boiling water, cover and bring back up to the boil. Remove the lid and boil, uncovered, for another 4-7 minutes until just cooked. While the asparagus is cooking, toast the bread and butter it. Remove the asparagus and place on the buttered toast. Drizzle with some of the hollandaise sauce and serve the rest in a jug on the table.

Pasta with Tomato and Ginger Salsa and Crème Fraîche

SERVES 4-6 / VEGETARIAN

The flavours in this sauce are lovely and very fresh. Ginger works surprisingly well with pasta, and the little bit of crème fraîche added at the end gives it a delicious creaminess.

400g (14oz) farfalle, penne or rigatoni, or something similar
15g (¹/₂oz) butter
2 spring onions, trimmed and sliced
10 ripe cherry tomatoes or 2 ripe tomatoes, roughly sliced
1 tsp finely grated ginger
Salt and freshly ground black pepper
Pinch of sugar
2-3 tbsp crème fraîche

Cook the pasta in boiling water according to the packet's instructions.

Meanwhile, heat the butter in a frying pan or wide saucepan, add the sliced spring onions and toss on the heat for a minutes until almost soft. Add the chopped tomatoes and the ginger, and season with salt and pepper and a good pinch of sugar. Toss in the pan on the heat for another couple of minutes until the tomatoes almost begin to soften. Then toss with the hot, drained pasta, add the crème fraîche, stir and serve.

Chicken Pie with Bacon and Peas

SERVES 8-10

My husband, Isaac, is an amazing cook, and this is one of his best weekend lunch dishes. It is so good and children love it too.

FOR THE FILLING:
1 chicken, about 2.25kg (5lb)
2 carrots, peeled and halved
1 celery stick, halved
1 onion, peeled and halved
Sprig of fresh thyme and fresh parsley
1 litre (1³/4 pints) water or light
　chicken stock
Salt and freshly ground black pepper
250ml (8fl oz) single cream
Roux (see page 215)
450g (1lb) button mushrooms,
　cut in half

25g (1oz) butter
400g (14oz) cooked ham, chopped
　into 2cm (3/4in) cubes
450g (1lb) peas
6 eggs, hard boiled for 10 minutes,
　peeled and chopped roughly
2 tbsp chopped fresh tarragon

FOR THE TOPPING:
400g (14oz) puff or flaky pastry,
　rolled to 5mm (1/4in) thick
1 egg, beaten, to glaze
Or
1.75kg (3³/4lb) mashed potato

Remove any giblets from inside the chicken and discard. Place the whole chicken in a large saucepan or casserole pot, add the carrots, celery, onion, thyme and parsley and the water or light chicken stock. Season with salt and pepper, cover with a lid and simmer for about 1¹/4 hours (or pop into a moderate oven) until the chicken is cooked. You will know when it is cooked as the leg will feel quite loose when you pull it from the carcass and the juices run clear when pierced.

If you have a pastry topping, preheat the oven to 230°C (450°F), Gas mark 8. For mashed potato, preheat the oven to 180°C (350°F), Gas mark 4.

Take the chicken out of the pot and set aside to cool for a few minutes. Remove the vegetables and herbs from the liquid in the pot and pour in the cream. Bring up to the boil, then whisk in some roux (about 2–3 tablespoons, but start with 1 tablespoon) until it has thickened slightly. The liquid must keep boiling while you add the roux in order to thicken.

Heat the butter in a pan over a high heat and fry the mushrooms for 4 minutes or until soft.

Remove the meat from the chicken carcass, chop roughly and place in a large pie dish (about 25 x 35cm (10 x 14in)), then add the chopped ham, peas (these can be straight from the freezer), chopped hard-boiled eggs, browned mushrooms and the chopped tarragon. Season to taste. If you are making this in advance, don't add the topping until just before you're ready to cook.

For a puff or flaky pastry top: cut the pastry to the same size as the top of the pie dish and arrange on top, making a hole in the centre to allow steam to escape. Brush the pastry with the beaten egg to give it a nice glaze. Cook it in the oven for 10 minutes, then turn down the oven to 190°C (375°F), Gas mark 5 and cook for another 20 minutes or until the pastry is golden brown and the mixture is bubbling hot.

For a mashed potato top: arrange the mashed potato on top of the chicken mixture and lightly score the surface. Place in the oven and cook for 30–40 minutes or until golden brown on top and bubbling hot.

Roast Leg of Lamb with Garlic and Rosemary and Olive Paste

SERVES 8-10

I love it when Isaac makes this for Sunday lunch. You can also serve it with Mint Sauce or Redcurrant Jelly (see pages 216 and 217).

FOR THE LAMB:
1 leg of lamb, about 2.5-3.25kg
   (5¹/₂-7¹/₄lb)
2 tbsp olive oil
1 tsp cracked black pepper (best if it is
   still a little coarse)
1 generous tbsp chopped rosemary
1 big pinch of sea salt
8 garlic cloves, peeled and sliced

FOR THE OLIVE PASTE:
100g (4oz) pitted black olives
1 tbsp capers
1 tsp Dijon mustard
1 tsp freshly squeezed lemon juice
Freshly ground black pepper
4 tbsp olive oil

Preheat the oven to 230°C (450°F), Gas mark 8. Using a very sharp knife, make about ten shallow slashes in criss-cross patterns on the top side of the meat. Mix together the olive oil, pepper, rosemary, sea salt and garlic and spread all over the lamb, pushing it into the incisions. Place it in a roasting tray and put it into the preheated oven.

Cook for 20 minutes, then turn the heat down to 180°C (350°F), Gas mark 4 and cook for a further 45 minutes for pink lamb, 1 hour 10 minutes for medium, or 1 hour 25 minutes for well-done. This cooking time allows 20 minutes per 500g (1lb 2oz) at this temperature. I usually aim for medium since there will inevitably be some pink bits and some well-done so that everyone can have their favourite!

To make the olive paste, whiz up the olives with the capers, mustard, lemon juice and pepper in a food processor – you probably won't need any salt. Add the olive oil. It keeps for months in a sterilised jar (see page 177) in the fridge.

When the lamb is cooked, allow it to rest for 15 minutes, covered with foil, somewhere warm if possible, then carve into slices and serve with the olive paste, mint sauce or redcurrant jelly.

Beef Stew with Brandy, White Wine and Cream

SERVES 10-12

This is such a good main course for entertaining, everyone always loves it. I usually make this quantity, even if I am just feeding six people, as it's useful having left overs for the next day or two.

500g (1lb 2oz) mushrooms, sliced
3-4 tbsp olive oil
3kg (7lb) stewing beef, cut into 3cm (1½in) cubes
150ml (5fl oz) chicken or beef stock
3 very large onions, peeled and sliced

5 garlic cloves, peeled and crushed
150ml (5fl oz) white wine
100ml (3½fl oz) brandy
325ml (11fl oz) single cream
Salt and freshly ground black pepper
2-3 tsp Roux (see page 215)

Preheat the oven to 160°C (325°F), Gas mark 3. Heat a large frying pan and sauté the mushrooms in batches in the olive oil until pale golden in colour. Tip onto a plate and set aside. Brown the meat in the same pan in small batches. When all the meat has browned, pour a small amount of the stock into the frying pan and bring to the boil to deglaze the pan and conserve the flavour.

Meanwhile, place a large flameproof casserole on the hob over a medium heat and pour the stock from the frying pan into it. Add the mushrooms, meat, sliced onions, garlic, white wine, stock and brandy. Cover with the lid, transfer to the oven and simmer for about 1-1½ hours or until tender.

When the meat is cooked, strain the liquid into a saucepan. Add the cream and boil uncovered for a few minutes until it has a good flavour, then season with salt and pepper.

With the liquid still boiling, add 2-3 teaspoons of the roux and whisk in until the juices have thickened slightly, adding more roux if necessary. Pour over the meat, stir and keep warm until you are ready to serve. Serve with Pilaff Rice (see page 218) or mashed potatoes.

Spaghetti with Beef, Olives, Capers and Anchovies
SERVES 6-8

This is a really good and gutsy pasta dish adapted from the classic pasta puttanesca (whores' pasta!). Leave out the beef if you wish. The sauce can be made in advance.

3-4 tbsp olive oil
575g (1lb 5oz) rump steak, cut into thin strips
2 onions, peeled and sliced
4 garlic cloves, peeled and crushed
1 x 410g tin chopped tomatoes (or 450g (1lb) of fresh tomatoes, peeled (see page 178) and chopped, reserving the juice)

Salt and freshly ground black pepper
Good pinch of sugar
25g (1oz) pitted black olives, chopped
25g (1oz) whole capers, rinsed if salted
12 whole anchovy fillets, roughly chopped
2 tbsp chopped tarragon or basil
600g (1lb 6oz) spaghetti

Heat half the olive oil in a pan, toss the meat for 30 seconds until brown, then remove from the pan and set aside. Add the remaining oil to the pan, and sweat the onion and garlic until soft. Add the tomatoes and their juices, salt and pepper and sugar. Cover with the lid and cook over a low heat for 10 minutes. Return the beef back to the sauce and allow it to simmer for a further 10 minutes or so until the sauce has thickened. Add the olives, capers, anchovies and chopped herbs, stir and set aside.

Cook the pasta in a large pot of boiling salted water until it is al dente. Drain and toss with the warm sauce and serve.

Gratin of Fish with Cheese, Tomatoes and Herbs

SERVES 6

Another great recipe of Isaac's! It is a terrifically easy and convenient main course and –
even better – it can be prepared in advance.

75g (3oz) Gruyère cheese, grated
75g (3oz) Emmental, grated (or a total of 150g (5oz) Gruyère instead)
3 generous tsp Dijon mustard
4–5 tbsp single cream
Salt and freshly ground black pepper
18 cherry tomatoes
1 generous tsp fresh thyme leaves or 1¹/₂ tbsp torn basil
750g (1lb 10oz) filleted and skinned flat-fish, such as plaice or lemon sole

Preheat the oven to 180°C (350°F), Gas mark 4. In a bowl, mix the grated cheese
with the mustard and cream, add a twist of black pepper and set aside. Cut the
cherry tomatoes in half, season with a little salt and sprinkle with the herbs.

Spread half the cheese mixture in a gratin dish (or individual ovenproof dishes).
Lay half the fish on top, then add all the tomatoes and herbs. Add the second
layer of fish, followed by the second layer of the cheese mixture. Place the dish
in the fridge until you are ready to cook it.

Cook in the preheated oven for 20–30 minutes (or 15 minutes for single portions)
until golden and bubbly. Serve with a big green salad and some boiled new
potatoes if you wish.

VARIATION

This dish can also be made using round, fleshy fish, such as haddock, cod or ling.
Use the same weight as the flat fish but place just one layer of fish in the dish.

Chocolate and Hazelnut Toffee Tart

SERVES 8-10 / VEGETARIAN

This is a really special and divinely rich tart, which is perfect served at the end of a meal with a cup of espresso or a glass of sweet dessert wine. It looks fantastic with its layers of sweet biscuity pastry underneath the hazelnut toffee, topped off with a rich and intense chocolate mousse.

1 x portion of **Sweet Shortcrust Pastry**
   (see page 221)
FOR THE HAZELNUT TOFFEE:
50g (2oz) butter
75ml (2³/4fl oz) single cream
100g (4oz) soft light brown sugar
150g (5oz) hazelnuts, roasted, peeled
   and coarsely chopped

FOR THE CHOCOLATE MOUSSE:
200ml (7fl oz) single cream
200g (7oz) dark chocolate, broken
   into pieces
TO SERVE:
Cocoa powder (optional)
Softly whipped cream

Roll out the pastry to line a 25cm (10in) tart tin (see page 220 for instructions). Cover and chill for 20 minutes, then blind bake (see also page 220). The pastry will not go into the oven again, so it must be completely cooked.

For the hazelnut toffee layer, place the butter, cream and brown sugar in a saucepan, bring to the boil and simmer for 2–3 minutes until slightly thickened. Remove from the heat, add the hazelnuts and allow it to cool. Spread over the cooked tart shell.

For the chocolate mousse, place the cream in a saucepan and bring to the boil, remove from the heat and immediately add the chocolate, stirring until the chocolate has melted and mixed with the cream. It should be just tepid now. Pour over the hazelnut toffee in the pastry case.

Place the tart somewhere cool until the chocolate mousse has set. If you are keeping it in the fridge, let it come back up to room temperature before you serve. Dust the tart with cocoa (if using), slice and serve with softly whipped cream.

Crème Brûlée Au Café

FILLS 4-5 ESPRESSO CUPS, SHOT GLASSES OR SMALL RAMEKINS / VEGETARIAN

Not many recipes come into my head as I sleep (unfortunately), but I woke up one morning having dreamt that I had eaten this in Italy. So when I tried it out later that day, I was delighted with the result! It's an excellent pudding to round-off a dinner party. The flavour of the coffee-infused custard is perfect with the 'burnt' sugar topping: divine inspiration! For the caramel topping you can use caster, granulated, light brown or dark brown sugar, but I have recommended light brown because the rich flavour works very well with the coffee custard. Since it is so rich it's best served in small portions. The custard needs to be made at least 5 hours in advance for it to set and be able to support the caramelised sugar top.

FOR THE CUSTARD:
1 generous tbsp ground coffee
   (not instant)
250ml (8fl oz) double cream

2 egg yolks
1 tbsp light brown sugar
FOR THE CARAMELISED TOPPING:
100g (4oz) light brown sugar

Place the coffee in a saucepan with the cream, bring up to just under boiling, then take off the heat and set aside for 1 minute to allow the coffee flavour to infuse. Pour through a very fine sieve into a bowl and wash out the saucepan.

Place the egg yolks and sugar in a bowl and whisk. Still whisking, add the coffee cream and mix completely. Pour this back into the clean, cool saucepan and place over a low heat. Stirring all the time, cook very slowly (it must not boil, otherwise it may scramble) until it thickens and can coat the back of a spoon – this will take a few minutes. Pour it immediately into serving cups, glasses or bowls and allow to cool, then place in the fridge for at least 5 hours (or overnight). Be careful not to break the skin on top or the caramel may sink later.

To prepare the caramel topping, place the sugar in a small saucepan over a medium heat and allow the sugar to caramelise, stirring all the time with a wooden spoon. It will look very lumpy and strange at first, but it will suddenly appear smooth, liquid and glossy. Immediately drizzle this caramel over the top of the custards. I like the custards to be just partially covered with the caramel. Do not swirl the custards while the caramel is being drizzled over as the skin may break and cause the caramel to sink. If using this method, the caramel can be made and poured on top of the custards about 5 or 6 hours in advance. Keep it somewhere dry so the caramel will not soften.

RACHEL'S HANDY TIP

If you have a cook's blow torch, you can sprinkle the set custards with a layer of sugar, about 1/2–1 teaspoon per portion. Light your blow torch and caramelise the sugar by holding the blow torch just a few centimetres from the cups until the sugar melts and bubbles. Allow to sit for 1 minute before serving. These can be finished a couple of hours before serving.

Amaretti Cookie Ice Cream with Hot Mocha Sauce

SERVES 6 / VEGETARIAN

This is the perfect dessert for the person who doesn't like to make either pastry or cakes. It's also great if you're in a hurry and want to make something fabulous with minimum effort. I love the rich, intense chocolate sauce with a hint of coffee and, if you like, you can leave out the brandy. The sauce can be prepared in advance (it will keep pretty much indefinitely in the fridge), just heat gently to serve.

FOR THE ICE CREAM:
400ml tub vanilla ice cream
100g (4oz) amaretti cookies,
    broken into chunks

FOR THE HOT MOCHA SAUCE:
100g (4oz) chocolate
100ml (3¹/₂fl oz) good strong coffee
    (can be left over from that morning!)
1 tbsp brandy (optional)

Take the ice cream out of the freezer and allow it to soften slightly, then add the broken amaretti cookies and fold into the ice cream. Cover and put back in the freezer until you are ready to serve.

To make the hot mocha sauce, melt the chocolate in a heatproof bowl in a low oven or microwave, or in a bowl set over a pan of simmering water. Take off the heat and whisk in the coffee and the brandy. Place a scoop or two of ice cream in a bowl, glass or cup and drizzle generously with the hot mocha sauce.

Little Hot After-dinner Shots

MAKES 8 / VEGETARIAN

Merrilees Parker, who is a great cook, made something similar to these when I appeared with her on *Great Food Live*. These are like little Irish coffees, only without the coffee!

200ml (7fl oz) brandy or whiskey
200ml (7fl oz) Stock Syrup (see page 221)
8 tbsp softly whipped cream

Place the brandy or whiskey in a saucepan with the stock syrup and heat very gently; do not boil. Divide between eight little glasses. Dip a spoon into boiling water and spoon on the cream, allowing it to slide off the spoon and sit on top of the sweet brandy or whiskey. The cream should not sink. Serve immediately.

6 Dining Alfresco

I absolutely adore eating alfresco.
You just can't beat gorgeous, lazy
days out in the garden with friends
and family, fun barbecues, a lunch
under an umbrella for shade, enjoying
breakfast while listening to the birds
and smelling the roses, romantic
candle-lit meals under the stars . . .
how lovely! I eat outdoors whenever
I get the chance, so that I can make
the most of our fairly brief but
warm summers.

Summer Omelette with Crispy Bacon, Tomato and Rocket Salad

SERVES 6

This is very much like an Italian frittata, with a gorgeous salad on top. It looks very pretty and dramatic on the table.

FOR THE OMELETTE:
4 tbsp olive oil
1 onion, peeled and chopped
Salt and freshly ground black pepper
8 eggs
100ml (3½fl oz) double cream
100ml (3½fl oz) milk
125g (4½oz) Gruyère or Parmesan cheese, grated
1-2 tbsp snipped fresh chives

FOR THE SALAD:
8 slices of streaky bacon, cooked in a pan until golden and crispy
6 ripe tomatoes, chopped into large chunks
1 tbsp olive oil
1-2 tsp lemon juice
Salt, freshly ground black pepper and sugar
50g (2oz) rocket leaves (2 big handfuls)

Make the omelette first. Heat a 28cm (11in) frying pan, add 2 tablespoons olive oil and the chopped onion, season and cook for 5-8 minutes, until almost soft and a little golden. Remove from the heat and allow to cool for a minute.

Whisk the eggs in a large bowl, add the cream, milk, the cooked onions, grated cheese and chopped chives; season to taste. Wipe out the frying pan, then heat it again and add another 2 tbsp olive oil, swirl it around, then pour in the egg mixture. Stir a couple of times, then cook over a low heat until it is golden and set underneath (about 10-15 minutes), then place under a hot grill to set the top (this may take another 4-5 minutes).

When cooked, flip or slide it out onto a large plate, and allow it to sit while you prepare the salad. It needs to cool slightly and to be eaten at room temperature.

To make the salad, slice the cooked bacon into 1cm (½in) pieces. Place in a bowl, add the tomatoes and drizzle with the olive oil and the lemon juice, season with salt, pepper and a pinch of sugar. When you are ready, toss the rocket leaves in very gently, then place on top of the omelette and serve.

This salad is also delicious made with smoked mackerel instead of the crispy bacon. Use 2-3 fillets of skinned smoked mackerel, cut into slices.

Asparagus Soldiers with Softly Boiled Eggs

SERVES 4 / VEGETARIAN

I love dipping spears of asparagus into softly boiled eggs, and they are great served up for an outdoor brunch. Do make sure you don't over-boil the eggs or it will be tricky to dip the asparagus into the yolk!

4 eggs
12 asparagus spears, woody ends snapped off

Hollandaise Sauce (see page 98)
Salt

Bring two saucepans of water up to the boil, one for the eggs and one for the asparagus. Boil the eggs in their shells for 4 minutes. While the eggs are boiling, cook the asparagus by dropping it into boiling water with a pinch of salt, cover and bring back up to the boil, then remove the lid and boil, uncovered, for 3-4 minutes until it is just cooked. Drain the eggs and the asparagus.

To eat, break open the 'lid' of your boiled egg, and dip the asparagus spears into the runny yolk.

Onion and Blue Cheese Tart

SERVES 6-8 / VEGETARIAN

Combined with a big green salad, this tart is perfect for an alfresco lunch in the garden. It is nice and easy to make, too, and there is no need to pre-cook the pastry.

FOR THE PASTRY:
250g (9oz) plain flour
125g (4¹/₂oz) butter
Pinch of salt
1 egg, beaten

FOR THE FILLING:
4 tbsp olive oil
3 very large onions, peeled and sliced
2 sprigs of fresh thyme or rosemary
Salt and freshly ground black pepper
100g (4oz) blue cheese, crumbled
    roughly into 1cm (¹/₂in) pieces

Make the pastry following the method on page 220 and allow it to rest in the fridge. Meanwhile, place the olive oil in a saucepan, add the sliced onions, herbs and salt and pepper. Stir, put on the lid and cook over a low heat for about 20 minutes, stirring regularly, until the onions are soft and tender. Discard the herb sprigs and pour out onto a plate to cool.

Roll out the chilled pastry between two sheets of cling film. When it is big enough to line a 20 x 30cm (8 x 12in) Swiss roll tin, remove the top layer of cling film and flip the pastry into the tin with the remaining sheet of cling film on top. Press it into the edges of the tin, remove the cling film and trim the edges. Using a fork, prick holes into the base of the pastry case. If you have time, it is best to allow the pastry to cool again before it goes into the oven to cook, so pop it into the freezer for 5 minutes if possible.

Preheat the oven to 180°C (350°F), Gas mark 4. Place a baking tray in the oven to heat up (this will help the base of the tart cook more evenly).

Pour the onions into the chilled pastry case, place on the hot baking tray in the oven and cook for 25-35 minutes until the pastry around the edge is crisp and golden. About 3 minutes before the end of the cooking time, sprinkle the tart with the crumbled blue cheese and pop back into the oven for another 3 minutes. The blue cheese will just begin to melt. Remove the tart from the oven and allow to cool slightly before sliding out onto a serving plate.

Nettle Soup

SERVES 6-8 / VEGETARIAN

People may not believe you when you say that you are making nettle soup, but it really is delicious. Even better, if your garden is anything like mine, the nettles are free and organic! Years ago, nettle soup was eaten to celebrate the arrival of spring, and this is the time to eat it as the young new shoots are the ones to pick. Just remember to wear your rubber gloves when picking them. To remove the formic acid (the part that gives them their sting), they do need to be cooked. This soup can also be served cold, like the Green Leaf and Pea Soup (see page 120), and with a little swirl of crème fraîche or thick natural yoghurt in the centre. If you don't have nettles to hand, you can use spinach, kale or watercress in their place.

25g (1oz) butter
1 potato, peeled and chopped
1 onion, peeled and chopped
Salt and freshly ground black pepper
600ml (1 pint) vegetable
   (or chicken) stock

600ml (1 pint) milk (add some single
   cream to this if you wish)
225g (8oz) nettle leaves,
   roughly chopped

Melt the butter in a saucepan, add the potatoes and onions, and season with salt and pepper. Cover and sweat on a gentle heat for 10 minutes, stirring every now and then. Take off the lid, add the stock and milk and bring to the boil. Cook until the potatoes are soft.

Add the nettles and boil, uncovered, over a high heat for just 2-3 minutes until the nettles have wilted. Do not overcook this soup or it will lose its fresh green colour and flavour. As soon as it is cooked, liquidise it. Taste and correct the seasoning and serve.

Green Leaf and Pea Soup

SERVES 6-8 / VEGETARIAN

My husband Isaac makes this in about 10 minutes flat. It can be served chilled as a nice starter on a hot day, or served hot for a cool summer's evening eating outside. Whether you are serving it cold or hot, it is also lovely to add a tiny blob of crème fraîche or a swirl of thick natural yoghurt in the centre.

1 litre (13/4 pints) vegetable (or chicken) stock
6 spring onions, trimmed and sliced
4 garlic cloves, peeled and crushed
Salt and freshly ground black pepper
450g (1lb) peas, fresh or frozen
250g (9oz) watercress, rocket or spinach, or a mixture of all three, roughly
    chopped and large stalks removed
200ml (7fl oz) single cream

Place the stock, spring onions and garlic in a saucepan, season with salt and pepper and bring to the boil. Boil for about 4 minutes, until the onions are soft, then add the peas and continue to boil over a high heat, removing the lid once the mixture comes to the boil.

After 1 minute, add the roughly chopped leaves and boil for a further 30 seconds–1 minute, until the peas and leaves are just tender. Add the cream and liquidise immediately. Then season to taste and serve.

Crab and Avocado Salad
SERVES 3-4

Not only is this a delicious salad, it is also great as a sandwich filling between two slices of really good brown or white bread.

200g (7oz) cooked crabmeat
1 tbsp Dijon mustard
1 tbsp Mayonnaise (see page 216)
2 tbsp chopped watercress

1 tbsp torn basil
1 ripe avocado, peeled,
   stoned and diced
Salt and freshly ground black pepper

Mix all the ingredients together and season to taste. Place on a lettuce leaf on a plate to serve for a starter or, if eating as a light main course, enjoy with some green salad and some bread on the side.

Avocado, Orange and Watercress Salad
SERVES 6 / VEGETARIAN

This salad has wonderful fresh flavours. It's great with spicy food, like South American Beef Steak with Chimichurri Salsa (see page 127). If you want to make this in advance, leave out the avocado and watercress until you are almost ready to serve.

50ml (2fl oz) olive oil
Juice of 1/2 lime
Sea salt and freshly ground
   black pepper
1 orange, peeled and chopped

2 avocados, halved, peeled, stoned
   and chopped roughly
125g (4 1/2oz) watercress sprigs
   (about 6 handfuls)

In a bowl mix the olive oil and lime juice and season with sea salt and freshly ground black pepper. Add the chopped orange and avocado. Then gently toss in the watercress sprigs and serve.

Warm Pasta Salad with Herbs, Garlic and Rocket Leaves

SERVES 4-6

This is perfect for alfresco eating; fresh and light and wonderful eaten either hot or just slightly warm. Leave out the chilli if you wish.

400g (14oz) pasta, like farfalle (pasta bows)
25g (1oz) butter
2 tbsp olive oil
4 cloves of crushed or grated garlic
1/2-1 red chilli, deseeded and finely chopped (optional)
2 generous tbsp chopped herbs (I use a mixture
of parsley, chives, basil and thyme)
20 cherry tomatoes, quartered
2 big handfuls of rocket leaves, left whole
Sea salt and freshly ground black pepper
50g (2oz) grated Parmesan cheese

Bring a large saucepan of salted water to the boil, add the pasta, and cook until al dente.

While the pasta is cooking, heat the butter and olive oil in a saucepan, add the garlic and chilli, and cook for about 20 seconds. Be careful not to burn the garlic.

Remove from the heat and add the chopped herbs, the quartered cherry tomatoes and the rocket leaves (they will wilt a bit from the heat). Season to taste with sea salt and freshly ground black pepper. Toss with the grated Parmesan and serve hot, or allow to cool and serve at room temperature.

South American Beef Steak with Chimichurri Salsa

SERVES 6

The flavours in the salsa marry beautifully with the steak, which can be cooked on a barbecue, in a frying pan or grill pan on the hob. It is delicious served with the Avocado, Orange and Watercress salad (see page 123).

6 sirloin steaks, about 1cm (1/2in) thick

FOR THE MARINADE:

6 garlic cloves, peeled and finely chopped

1 red chilli, deseeded and finely chopped

Juice of 1 orange

Juice of 1 lemon

2 tbsp chopped fresh parsley

100ml (3 1/2fl oz) olive oil

FOR THE CHIMICHURRI SALSA:

1 garlic clove, peeled and finely chopped

1 tbsp finely chopped spring onion

1 tbsp white wine vinegar

1 pinch of dried chilli flakes

2 tbsp chopped fresh coriander

2 tbsp chopped fresh parsley

Juice of 1/2 lime

100ml (3 1/2fl oz) olive oil

Salt and freshly ground black pepper

Using a sharp knife score the steaks 1mm (1/16in) deep in a criss-cross pattern. Combine the ingredients for the marinade in a shallow glass or china dish or strong plastic bag, add the beef and toss in the marinade. Then place in the fridge for at least 1 hour (or up to about 8 hours).

To make the salsa, combine all the ingredients in a bowl and season to taste with salt and pepper.

Heat a grill pan, frying pan or your barbecue until very hot. Remove the beef from the marinade and cook for about 3–4 minutes on each side or longer, depending on your taste. Reserve the marinade and use it to brush over the steaks during cooking. Transfer to serving plates, spoon over the chimichurri salsa, with more in a bowl on the side, and serve.

Fruity Cocktails

MAKES 2-4 / VEGETARIAN

These are all really refreshing cocktails to have on a summer's evening with friends.

CAMPARI AND GRAPEFRUIT FIZZ

5 tbsp Stock Syrup (see page 221)
1 tbsp Campari
125ml (4fl oz) grapefruit juice
200ml (7fl oz) sparkling white wine

Place the syrup, Campari and grapefruit juice in a jug and stir. Add the sparkling wine and pour into chilled champagne or wine glasses.

COOL CAMPARI AND LIME GIN AND TONIC

75ml (2³/4fl oz) gin
25ml (1fl oz) Campari
Juice of 1 lime (or ¹/2 lemon)
200ml (7fl oz) crushed ice
100ml (3¹/2fl oz) tonic

Pour the gin, Campari and lime or lemon juice into a jug. Add the crushed ice, stir to mix, then add the tonic water. Serve in whiskey tumblers or strain into cocktail glasses.

STRAWBERRY OR RASPBERRY DAIQUIRI

150ml (5fl oz) white rum or vodka
250g (9oz) strawberries or raspberries (can be frozen)
75ml (2³/4fl oz) lime juice (approximately 3 limes)
100-125ml (3¹/2-4fl oz) Stock Syrup (see page 221), to taste
Crushed ice, to serve

Place the rum, strawberries (or raspberries), lime juice and 100ml (3¹/2fl oz) stock syrup in a blender and whiz until smooth. Taste and add more stock syrup if necessary. Pour into tumblers half-filled with crushed ice.

Summer Tiramisu

SERVES 10-12 / VEGETARIAN

This is such a great dessert to serve when you have lots of people over for a big get-together. My friend, Clare Pocock, made this gorgeous tiramisu and brought it along to a big extended family barbecue and everyone loved it.

150ml (5fl oz) water
200g (7oz) unbleached caster sugar
400g (14oz) mixed berries (fresh or frozen)
50ml (2fl oz) crème de cassis or crème de framboise
4 eggs, separated
250g tub mascarpone cheese
1 x 200g packet boudoir biscuits (sponge biscuits)
50g (2oz) flaked or slivered almonds

Make a syrup by dissolving half the sugar in the water, then boiling for 2 minutes. Add in the fruit. If using fresh fruit, turn off the heat and leave it to cool. If using frozen fruit, bring the syrup back to the boil and let it simmer very gently for 1–2 minutes, then leave to cool. Add the cassis or frambroise to the syrup.

Beat the egg yolks in a bowl with the remaining sugar until pale and thick. Beat in the mascarpone cheese. In a separate bowl, whisk the egg whites until they form stiff peaks. Fold them lightly into the egg and mascarpone mixture.

Strain the fruit from the syrup. Place the syrup in a wide bowl. Dip half the biscuits in the cooled syrup and use them to line the base of a 28cm (11in) gratin dish. Spread half the mascarpone mixture over, followed by half the fruit. Cover the fruit with another layer of the biscuits dipped in the liquid. Spread over the remainder of the fruit, followed by the remaining mascarpone mixture. Cover and chill for a minimum of 6 hours, or ideally overnight, to allow the biscuits to absorb the juices and soften.

Meanwhile, toast the almonds by heating a dry frying pan, tossing in the nuts and frying for 2–3 minutes until golden. Set aside to cool. Use to sprinkle over the tiramisu just prior to serving.

Custard Tart

SERVES 6-8 / VEGETARIAN

This is quite simply a tasty and light, old-fashioned tart.

1 x 25cm (10in) sweet pastry shell (see page 221),
  blind baked
475ml (16fl oz) milk
3 eggs
50g (2oz) caster sugar
1 tsp vanilla extract or essence
Pinch of ground nutmeg or cinnamon

Preheat the oven to 180°C (350°F), Gas mark 4. Place the blind baked pastry shell in its tin on a baking tray.

Heat the milk to just under boiling point. Whisk the eggs in a bowl, add the sugar and vanilla and whisk. Then whisk in the hot milk. To avoid spills, place the empty pastry shell on the oven shelf and very carefully pour in the custard. Close the oven door and cook for 10 minutes, then open the oven door and sprinkle the top of the tart with the ground nutmeg or cinnamon and bake for another 10 minutes, or until it is just set in the centre. Remove from the oven and allow to cool a little before removing from the tin. It will set a little more as it cools. Cut into slices and serve.

RACHEL'S HANDY TIP

To remove the tart from a loose-bottomed tin, make sure that the pastry is not stuck to sides of the tin, then place the tin on a small bowl or cup and the outer ring part should fall down. Then lift the tart slightly and remove the ring and the bowl. If you are feeling confident you can remove the base of the tin by sliding a palette knife or a fish slice between the pastry and the base of the tin, and sliding the tart onto your chosen plate. Alternatively, just leave the tart on the tin base.

Baked Meringue with Peaches

SERVES 6 / VEGETARIAN

A past student at the cookery school, Jo Jessop, who comes from South Highlands, Australia, gave me this recipe. It's wonderful served with vanilla ice cream; the hot baked meringue with the frozen ice cream works very well in that 'baked Alaska' kind of way. It is just as easy to make this for 26 as it is for six, provided you have a large enough gratin dish!

4 peaches or nectarines
25g (1oz) brown sugar
2 tbsp Marsala, sweet sherry or lemon juice
4 egg whites
250g (9oz) light brown sugar or caster sugar

Preheat the oven to 180°C (350°F), Gas mark 4. Cut the peaches in half (there's no need to peel them) and remove the stones. Slice the peaches about 5mm (1/4in) thick and lay in a 1.25 litre (2 1/4 pint) pie dish. Sprinkle with brown sugar and drizzle with the Marsala, sherry or lemon juice. If the peaches are not very ripe and juicy (although they should be ripe enough to eat), pop them into the oven for 5 minutes to cook, while you make the meringue. If they are very ripe and juicy there is no need to do this.

To make the meringue, whisk the egg whites in a bowl with an electric beater until stiff. Still beating, gradually add the light brown sugar and continue to beat until the meringue holds stiff peaks. Spoon the meringue on top of the peaches and cook in the preheated oven for 15–20 minutes, or until the meringue feels slightly firm in the centre and is a deep golden colour on top.

7 Home Cinema

Cooking for an evening of home cinema is such fun. It is the perfect excuse to indulge and eat sticky, gooey treats in front of the telly, all snuggled up under a blanket watching your favourite flicks. The only trick is to make sure you prepare food that can either be eaten with your hands, or food that is all on the one plate and not awkward to eat, or else you'll be forever picking bits off the sofa, your lap, or each other!

Baked Potatoes

A baked potato is the perfect food to eat while watching a good movie. Whether your favourite topping is baked beans or Manchego cheese with Serrano ham, there is always something in the fridge for everyone. Baked potatoes are good and wholesome because most of the goodness in a potato is stored just under the skin, which is retained when you bake it – none of it is lost in cooking water.

1 large potato per person in its skin, scrubbed clean

Preheat the oven to 230°C (450°F), Gas mark 8. Pierce a few holes in the potato with a skewer or a fork and put on a tray or rack into the preheated oven. Cook for 40–55 minutes, until the potato feels soft under the crispy skin. You can cook the potatoes with a metal skewer stuck through them to speed up the cooking process. When the potato is baked, remove it from the oven and cut a cross in it to open it out slightly. Serve with a topping of your choice – each of those given here (there are two more overleaf) makes enough for two potatoes.

SERRANO HAM AND MANCHEGO CHEESE WITH WALNUT DRESSING
2 slices Serrano ham (or Parma ham)
4 slices of Manchego cheese, or Parmesan cheese
FOR THE WALNUT DRESSING:
1 tbsp walnut oil
1 generous tsp white wine vinegar
1/4 tsp Dijon mustard
Salt and freshly ground black pepper

Shake all the dressing ingredients together in a jar with a screw-top lid. Drape a slice of Serrano ham and a couple of thin slices of Manchego cheese over the top of each opened potato. Drizzle with a teaspoon or two of the walnut dressing.

GRUYÈRE CHEESE AND CRISPY BACON
2 tbsp bacon lardons, 1 x 2cm ($^{1}/_{2}$ x $^{3}/_{4}$in) in size
15g ($^{1}/_{2}$oz) butter
4 tbsp grated Gruyère cheese
Freshly ground black pepper

Cook the lardons in a hot pan until crispy. Dot each potato with the butter, sprinkle with the crispy bacon, the grated cheese and a little black pepper, and pop it back into the hot oven for 3–4 minutes until the cheese is melted and bubbling.

SMOKED SALMON
50g (2oz) smoked salmon (for 2 people)
15g ($^{1}/_{2}$oz) capers, rinsed then dried in kitchen paper
10g ($^{1}/_{4}$oz) butter or $^{1}/_{2}$ tbsp olive oil
Freshly ground black pepper
Squeeze of lemon juice
2 tbsp crème fraîche
Handful of snipped fresh chives

Cut the salmon into little lardons and toss with the capers in the butter or olive oil in a hot pan. Add the pepper and a squeeze of lemon juice. Add a good tablespoon of crème fraîche onto the split cooked potatoes, sprinkle with the salmon and capers and decorate with chopped chives.

Yummy Dips

EACH DIP SERVES 4-6 PEOPLE / VEGETARIAN

I love having a selection of dips on a home-cinema night. Tortilla chips (bought, or homemade and baked) are great for dipping, as are roast potato wedges or even, dare I say, raw vegetable sticks (but only if I am feeling very good and virtuous). These dips can all be made in advance, and their individual flavours work well with each other.

HUMMUS
1 x 400g tin of chickpeas, drained, or 200g (7oz) dried chickpeas
Juice of $1/2$-1 lemon
2 garlic cloves, peeled and crushed

3-4 tbsp olive oil
2 generous tbsp tahini paste (sesame seed paste)
Salt and freshly ground black pepper
2 tbsp natural yoghurt (optional)

If using dried chickpeas, soak them in water overnight, then drain and cook in fresh water for about 45 minutes, or until soft. Drain again and allow to cool. Put all the ingredients into a food processor and pulse until smooth. Check for seasoning, add more olive oil or some natural yoghurt if it is too thick. This keeps in the fridge for up to a week.

TOMATO AND CUCUMBER SALSA
16 cherry tomatoes, or 4 red ripe tomatoes, finely chopped
$1/4$ cucumber, deseeded and finely chopped
2 garlic cloves, peeled and crushed

$1/2$ small red onion, peeled and finely chopped
1-2 tbsp lemon or lime juice
1-2 tbsp chopped mint
Salt and freshly ground black pepper

Mix all the ingredients in a bowl and season to taste.

CRÈME FRAÎCHE WITH SWEET CHILLI
6 tbsp crème fraîche
2 tbsp sweet chilli sauce

Mix together the ingredients, adding more sweet chilli sauce if you like.

Toasted Ham and Gruyère Sandwich

MAKES 1 SANDWICH

This is a classic combination, and I think it makes the ultimate TV supper. This recipe makes enough for one sandwich, but you can easily make more for a crowd!

2 slices of white bread, ciabatta or sourdough bread
Softened butter
2 slices of ham or, even better, glazed bacon
2–3 slices of Gruyère cheese
1 tbsp wholegrain or Dijon mustard

Lay the slices of bread on a work top. Spread one slice with butter, add a layer of ham, then the Gruyère cheese. Spread the other slice of bread with the mustard and place on top of the ham, mustard-side-down. Spread some butter on the top of the sandwich.

Place a frying pan on the heat and straight away put the sandwich in the pan, butter-side-down. Place a saucepan lid on the pan and cook over a medium heat for about 3–4 minutes, until golden on the underside. Spread a tiny bit of butter on the top and flip over. Cover again, turn down the heat and cook for another 3–4 minutes until golden and the cheese is just melted. Remove from the pan and serve.

RACHEL'S HANDY TIP
To make a lot of these I would cook the sandwiches in a hot oven for 8–10 minutes, which is far more convenient than cooking them one by one in a frying pan.

Lamb Samosas

MAKES 20

I love it when Isaac makes these for a night in front of the flicks. Samosas are the ultimate finger food, which makes them the ultimate telly food! Use filo pastry as a faster alternative to the traditional samosa pastry. For a vegetarian version, replace the lamb with an equal quantity of boiled, skinned and chopped potato.

2 tbsp sunflower or olive oil
300g (11oz) finely chopped
   or minced lamb
1 onion, peeled and chopped
1 tsp ground cumin
1 tsp ground coriander
Salt and freshly ground black pepper

100g (4oz) peas (fresh or frozen)
1 tbsp chopped fresh coriander
5 sheets of filo pastry, measuring
   25 x 50cm (10 x 20in)
1 egg, beaten

Heat a frying pan, add the sunflower or olive oil, then toss in the lamb, onion and ground spices. Season and cook for about 10 minutes without a lid until the lamb is just cooked and the juices have evaporated. Add the peas and toss. Take off the heat and add the chopped coriander and season again to taste. Set aside for a minute to let the lamb cool.

Meanwhile, lay the filo pastry out on a board and cut into half lengthways, then into half widthways, so you have four rectangles from each whole sheet. Cover all the pieces of filo with a barely damp tea towel (to prevent them from drying out). Place one sheet lengthways in front of you and pile a dessertspoon of the lamb mixture at the end closest to you. Roll the pastry from the end closest to you, once, then fold in both the long sides and then roll over and over, away from you, into a little parcel. Brush the finishing edge with a little of the beaten egg to seal and then place on a baking tray. Brush the finished samosa with beaten egg and repeat with all the remaining pastry and meat.

These can be prepared earlier in the day up to this point and chilled in the fridge. To cook, place the baking tray into an oven preheated to 220°C (425°F), Gas mark 7 for 10-12 minutes until golden.

Creamy Tomatoes on Toast

SERVES 2 / VEGETARIAN

My mum used to make this for us when we came home from school and I still adore it. This is great, easy food to have in front of the television.

200ml (7fl oz) single cream
1 sprig of fresh rosemary or 2 sprigs of fresh thyme
1 garlic clove, peeled and chopped
4 ripe tomatoes, cut in half
Sea salt and freshly ground black pepper
2-4 slices of white yeast or soda bread
About 2 tbsp olive oil

Preheat the oven to 200°C (400°F), Gas mark 6. In a saucepan, simmer the cream with the herbs and garlic for 5 minutes until it has thickened slightly.

Place the tomatoes cut-side-up in a gratin or ovenproof dish and pour over the cream with garlic and herbs. Season with salt and pepper and then bake in the oven for 15–20 minutes or until the tomatoes are soft and blistered and the cream is thick and reduced.

Meanwhile, drizzle the bread with a little of the olive oil and pop into the oven for the last 5 minutes of the cooking time. When the toast and tomatoes are cooked, remove from the oven. Place the toast on warm plates and divide the tomato halves out between the toast, then spoon any cream left in the gratin dish over the top and serve.

Raclette

SERVES 4

Raclette is both the name of a semi-soft Savoyard cheese and a traditional dish in which slices of the cheese were put on the hearth near a glowing fire. Diners would gather around with plates, knives and forks in hand and a bowl of boiled potatoes. As the cheese melts, it is scraped off, spread across the potatoes and eaten with gusto! Today, most people use electric raclette machines at the table and each diner helps themselves to cheese to melt on their own little handled tray under the raclette grill, which they then enjoy with hot boiled potatoes, a selection of charcuterie, cornichons and tomatoes. Similar to a cheese fondue, it's great fun for a big casual supper party, or amazing to enjoy in front of a good movie – slide a low coffee table near to the sofa on which to stand the raclette machine.

8–12 floury potatoes
500g (1lb 2oz) Raclette cheese, cut into slices 5mm (¼in) thick
A selection of charcuterie
Ripe tomatoes
Cornichons, sliced
Cucumber Pickle (see page 174)
A chutney such as Spicy Tomato and Apple Chutney (see page 179) or Onion Marmalade (see page 181)
Sea salt and black pepper in a mill

Plug in the raclette machine and allow it to heat up. Boil the potatoes until soft.

Put the cheese, charcuterie, tomatoes, cornichons, cucumber pickle and relishes on plates or in bowls. When the potatoes have boiled, place them in a warm bowl on the table. Let each guest take a slice of cheese and place it under the grill on the raclette machine. While the cheese is melting, let everyone help themselves to all the other ingredients on the table. Split open a potato and when the cheese is melted and bubbling, scrape it onto the potato and enjoy.

Popcorn Paradise

SERVES 4 / VEGETARIAN

It is difficult to have a home-cinema night without popcorn, so why not try this recipe and all its variations? Serve the popcorn in a big bowl or in paper cornets for each person.

PLAIN POPCORN
3 tbsp sunflower oil
75g (3oz) popcorn
25g (1oz) butter
Pinch of salt

Heat the oil in a medium saucepan. Add the popcorn and swirl the pan to coat the popcorn in oil. Turn down the heat to low, cover, and the corn should start to pop in a couple of minutes. As soon as it stops popping (after 5–7 minutes), take the saucepan off the heat and add the butter and salt. Put the lid back on the pan and shake to mix. Pour out into bowls and leave to cool a little.

VARIATIONS

TOFFEE POPCORN
Cook the popcorn as for the plain popcorn recipe, but while the corn is popping, make the toffee coating by melting 25g (1oz) butter in a small saucepan. Then add 25g (1oz) brown sugar and 1 generous tablespoon golden syrup and stir over a high heat for 1/2–1 minute until thick. Pour the toffee over the popcorn, put the lid on the pan and shake to mix. Pour out into bowls and cool a little before serving.

SPICED POPCORN
Cook the popcorn as for the plain popcorn recipe as far as removing the pan from the heat. In a bowl, mix 1 1/2 teaspoons each of ground cumin and coriander seeds with 1/2 teaspoon each of medium-strength curry powder and ground paprika and 3/4 teaspoon ground cayenne pepper. Heat 2 teaspoons sunflower oil in a frying pan, add the spices and stir for about 30 seconds until lightly toasted. Throw in 25g (1oz) caster sugar and 3/4 teaspoon salt, stir, then add all of this into the popped popcorn in the saucepan, toss and empty into a big bowl.

8 Big Celebrations

From time to time we all find ourselves in a situation where we need to cook for lots of people – it could be for a big birthday or anniversary party, or maybe even an informal party after a wedding. On such occasions, the food needs to be something that can be prepared in advance, food that is easy to serve, and food with ingredients that everyone will like. To top it all, the food must also be just as easy to make for 26 as it is for 16 or even six! So hopefully you'll find lots of inspiration in this chapter.

Green Salad with Honey Mustard Dressing

SERVES ABOUT 20 PEOPLE / VEGETARIAN

There can be nothing easier to prepare for a large gathering than a bowl filled with a beautiful combination of your favourite salad ingredients. A green salad doesn't have to be bland and uninteresting. It all depends on the leaves that you use (a good selection will give a lovely range of colours and flavours – try edible flowers too!), and the oil in the dressing. Try to use as good an olive oil as you can afford and it will make all the difference.

FOR THE GREEN SALAD:

As large a selection as possible of edible leaves and herbs

Edible flowers, such as wild garlic, nasturtium, edible chrysanthemum and chive

FOR THE DRESSING:

3 tbsp olive oil (use your best extra-virgin for this)

1 tbsp white wine vinegar

1 tsp wholegrain mustard

1 tsp honey

1 large garlic clove, peeled and crushed

Sprig of parsley

A few chives, trimmed and chopped

Salt and freshly ground black pepper

Wash and dry the leaves and flowers and then tear them into bite-sized pieces. Put into a plastic bag or a covered bowl, which can be stored in the fridge for a couple of days if you need to get ahead. This is particularly good if you buy or pick all your leaves in one go or you have friends staying for the weekend. You can then just pick and choose whatever you need, whenever you need it.

To make the dressing, place all the ingredients in a jar with a lid and shake to mix. Taste for seasoning. Drizzle sparingly over a selection of your prepared salad ingredients in a bowl and toss to serve.

Chicken Pilaff

SERVES 6

This is a great main course for feeding lots of people and can be made in advance.
It's a firm favourite of adults and children alike. For large gatherings, double or treble
the quantities.

1 large chicken, about 2.5kg (5½lb)
1 carrot, peeled and halved
1 onion, peeled and halved
6 whole black peppercorns
Large sprig of parsley
Large sprig of thyme

750ml (1¼ pints) chicken stock
250ml (8fl oz) white wine
Salt and freshly ground black pepper
250ml (8fl oz) single cream
2–3 tbsp Roux (see page 215)

Preheat the oven to 160°C (325°F), Gas mark 3. Remove any giblets from the
chicken carcass and place the chicken in a large saucepan or casserole. Add the
carrot, onion, peppercorns, herbs, stock and white wine and bring up to the boil.
Season with salt and pepper, cover with the lid and place in the preheated oven
to cook for 1½–2 hours or until the chicken is completely cooked. I test this by
pulling the leg – if it feels as though it will come away from the carcass easily and
the juices run clear when pierced, then it is ready. (For a larger chicken, cook for
20 minutes per 450g (1lb) plus 30 minutes.)

Remove the chicken from the stock and place it on a large plate. Remove all the
meat from the carcass, discarding the skin and bones. Cut the chicken into strips
approximately 1cm (½in) wide and 5cm (2in) long. Cover and keep warm.

Remove the vegetables, peppercorns and herbs from the liquid and discard. Add
the cream, bring up to the boil and boil uncovered for a few minutes. If the flavour
is a little weak, boil for longer, then season to taste. While still boiling, whisk in the
roux – you need enough to thicken it so it just about coats the back of a spoon.

Place the chicken and any juices back in the casserole, once again correcting
the seasoning, and keep warm until needed. Serve with Pilaff Rice (see page 218),
mashed potatoes or boiled new potatoes and the Green Salad with Honey
Mustard Dressing (see page 150).

Moroccan Lamb Tagine with Lemon and Pomegranate Couscous

SERVES 12-14

This is one of those great dishes that is perfect for small dinner parties and big celebrations alike. It's very straightforward to prepare and is so, so delicious!

4 tbsp olive oil
8 garlic cloves, peeled and crushed
4 onions, peeled and chopped
4 tsp grated ginger
1¹/₂ tbsp coriander seeds, crushed
3 tsp cumin seeds, crushed
3 tsp ground cinnamon
Salt and freshly ground black pepper
3kg (7lb) shoulder of lamb, boned, fat discarded and cut into 4cm (1¹/₂in) cubes
2 tbsp tomato paste

2kg (4¹/₂lb) ripe tomatoes or 4 x 400g tins tomatoes, coarsely chopped
4-5 tbsp honey
Wedges of lime and a bowl of Greek yoghurt, to serve

FOR THE COUSCOUS:

1 large or 2 small pomegranates
800g (1³/₄lb) couscous
6 tbsp olive oil
Juice of 2 lemons
1 litre (1³/₄ pints) boiling chicken stock or water
4 tbsp chopped fresh mint or coriander

Preheat the oven to 160°C/325°F/Gas mark 3. Heat a large flameproof casserole or heavy saucepan, add the olive oil, garlic, onions, ginger and spices. Season with salt and pepper, stir and cook on a low heat with the lid on for about 10 minutes, until the onions are soft.

Add the lamb, tomato paste, chopped tomatoes and honey. Stir it all together, bring to a simmer and place in the oven for 1¹/₂ hours, until the lamb is tender and cooked. Remove the lid halfway through cooking to let the liquid reduce and thicken. Season to taste. If it is still a bit thin, put the dish or saucepan on the hob on a medium heat and without the lid. Stir occasionally and let the liquid thicken.

Cut the pomegranate in half. Scoop out the seeds using a teaspoon and remove the white membrane. Place the couscous in a bowl and mix in the olive oil and lemon juice. Pour in the boiling stock or water and season. Allow to sit in a warm place for 5-10 minutes until the liquid is absorbed. To serve, stir in the chopped herbs and pomegranate seeds. Place the tagine on serving plates with couscous and a wedge of lime, and place a bowl of thick yoghurt in the middle of the table.

Thai Pork with Coconut Coriander Sauce

SERVES 10-12

This is a delicious recipe with mild South-east Asian flavours. The dish keeps very well if you make it in advance; just keep the cooked pork in a saucepan with the sauce, which will prevent the meat from drying out. Heat it up gently when you're ready to serve it.

2kg (4½lb) pork fillet (tenderloin), trimmed (about 4 fillets)

FOR THE MARINADE:

4 tbsp roughly chopped fresh coriander leaves and stalks

10 spring onions, trimmed

3cm (1¼in) piece of fresh ginger, peeled and chopped

8 garlic cloves, peeled

Finely grated zest and juice of ½ lemon

1 red chilli, deseeded and roughly chopped

2 stalks of lemon grass, trimmed and outer leaves discarded

4 tbsp brown sugar

4 tbsp soy sauce

4 tbsp fish sauce (nam pla)

4 tbsp sesame oil

FOR THE SAUCE:

2 x 400ml tins coconut milk

2 tbsp fish sauce (nam pla)

2 tbsp lemon juice

1-2 tbsp chopped fresh coriander leaves and stalks

Salt and freshly ground black pepper

Cut the pork at an angle into slices 1cm (½in) thick, so that you have oval slices about 10cm (4in) long and 6cm (2½in) wide.

Make the marinade by placing the coriander, spring onions, ginger, garlic, lemon zest, chilli and lemon grass in a food processor and whiz until you have a fine paste. Put into a bowl and add the remainder of the marinade ingredients. (If whizzing in a liquidiser, simply whiz all the marinade ingredients together.) Add the slices of pork and toss in the marinade. Cover and place in the fridge until you are ready to cook the meat (for at least 30 minutes, or even overnight if you wish).

Heat a frying pan or grill pan until it is almost smoking, remove the pork from the marinade (reserving the marinade for the sauce) and cook the pork in a single layer over a high heat for 1-2 minutes or until golden underneath. Turn and continue to cook until the meat is cooked through. If you are cooking lots of meat, you can just toss for 1 minute on each side in the pan, then transfer it to a roasting tray and cook in a hot oven preheated to 220°C (425°F), Gas mark 7 for another 5 minutes or until it is cooked through.

While the pork is cooking, place the reserved marinade in a small saucepan. Add the coconut milk, bring up to the boil and boil uncovered for about 5 minutes until it has thickened a little. Add the fish sauce, lemon juice and chopped coriander and season to taste with more fish sauce or lemon juice if necessary. The fish sauce is quite salty so you might not need any additional salt.

Serve the pork on a bed of Thai Rice (see page 219) or Plain Boiled Rice (see page 218) with some sauce on top or in a bowl on the side.

RACHEL'S HANDY TIP
This main course also works very well as a canapé. Just cut the pork into small cubes about 2cm (3/4in) square and thread onto cocktail sticks (or small satay sticks) that have been soaking in water for 1 hour. Cook on a barbecue or in a frying pan for 6 minutes on each side and serve with a bowl of the coconut coriander sauce in the centre of the plate.

Thai Stir-fried Beef with Red Peppers and Pak Choy

SERVES 16

This is a great stir-fry that can be prepped in advance and then cooked when you are nearly ready to serve. I love to serve this with noodles or rice and some wedges of lime for each person to squeeze over their own plateful.

2.4kg (5¼lb) rump or sirloin steak, trimmed and thinly sliced across the grain
8 tbsp fish sauce (nam pla)
8 tbsp oyster sauce
8 large garlic cloves, peeled and chopped
8 tbsp sunflower oil or vegetable oil
6 large red peppers, quartered, deseeded and finely sliced
8 heads pak choy, root end trimmed, then sliced across about 1cm (½in) thick
4-6 small chillies, deseeded and chopped
8 tbsp roughly chopped basil (only chop when you need it as it goes black if chopped in advance)
Lime wedges, to serve

Place the sliced beef in a bowl, add half the fish sauce, half the oyster sauce and half the chopped garlic. Stir to mix and leave to marinate in the fridge for 1–2 hours if possible, or even longer if you can.

Heat half the oil in a wok (or large frying pan), add the red pepper and toss over the heat for a couple of minutes, then add the pak choy. Keep tossing over the heat until just tender, then add the remaining garlic and the chillies. Cook for another 10 seconds, then remove from the heat and set aside.

Heat the remaining oil in the wok or pan, and when it is very hot, add the beef, drained from any marinade (reserve the marinade for later). Cook for 2 minutes, stirring all the time, or until cooked through.

Return the vegetables to the wok, add the remaining fish sauce, oyster sauce and marinade and toss over the heat for 30 seconds. Taste and add more fish sauce and oyster sauce if you wish. Remove from the heat and stir in the roughly chopped basil, and serve immediately with a wedge of lime on the side of each plate and with steamed rice or noodles.

Beef with Prunes and Peppers

SERVES 20

This recipe of my friend, Iona Murray, is absolutely great for serving lots and lots of people. It is best made several hours in advance or even the day before, which makes it very handy for entertaining. The prunes seem to dissolve and give the sauce a sweet richness.

3.5kg (8lb) chuck/stewing beef, trimmed and cut into 2cm (3/4in) chunks
3–4 tbsp olive oil
Salt and freshly ground black pepper
3 large onions, peeled and chopped
6 fat garlic cloves, peeled
1 x 75cl bottle of red wine
8–10 red peppers, deseeded and chopped

Large bunch of thyme, tied together
3–4 fresh bay leaves
350g (12oz) pitted ready-to-eat prunes, cut in half
Zest of 1 large orange, pared and thinly sliced, and then juice the orange
4 red chillies, deseeded and chopped
4 tbsp tomato purée
1 cinnamon stick
Roux (see page 215) (optional)

Preheat the oven to 160°C (325°F), Gas mark 3. Trim the meat and put it in a large bowl. Pour over 1–2 tablespoons of the olive oil and season with salt and pepper.

Heat a frying pan over a high flame and brown all the meat in batches. Remove the meat from the pan and place in a large saucepan or casserole. Add some more olive oil to the pan and toss the onions and garlic on a high heat for a minute, then transfer to the casserole. With the frying pan still on the heat, pour some of the wine into it and stir around for a minute; this will deglaze the frying pan. Pour into the casserole.

Add the peppers, thyme, bay leaves, prunes, orange zest and juice, the chillies, the remaining wine, the tomato purée and the cinnamon stick, mix again and bring to the boil. Season and cover with a well-fitting lid and place in the oven. Cook for about 2 hours, until the meat is meltingly tender and you can cut it with a fork. If it is looking dry, add some water or light stock.

When it is done, remove from the oven and allow to cool. If the sauce is too runny, put a ladleful in a small saucepan, bring to the boil and whisk in some roux, return to the main dish and mix in. Or if the sauce is too dry, add a bit of stock or water to get the desired consistency. Serve with rice or mashed potatoes.

Roast Southeast Asian Salmon
SERVES 12-15

This is such a great main course for a big dinner party or family gathering.

2 fresh salmon fillets, each weighing
   1-1.25kg (2-2½lb)
Salt and freshly ground black pepper
FOR THE SAUCE:
150ml (5fl oz) fish sauce (nam pla)
150ml (5fl oz) white wine

2 garlic cloves, peeled and crushed
3 tsp finely grated ginger
2 tbsp brown sugar
Juice of 2 small limes
1 handful chopped fresh coriander

Preheat the oven to 200°C (400°F), Gas mark 6. Place the fish, skin-side-down, on an oiled piece of tin foil on a baking tray. Fold up the edges slightly to make a wall around the fish and season with salt and pepper.

Mix together the fish sauce, white wine, garlic, ginger and brown sugar in a saucepan and boil uncovered for about 5 minutes or until slightly thickened. Pour half of the sauce over the fish and cook in the oven for 20 minutes, or until the fish is cooked.

When the fish is cooked, transfer to a serving plate. Add the lime juice and chopped coriander to the remaining sauce and spoon over the hot salmon. Serve with noodles or rice. This dish is also delicious served at room temperature with salads.

Vietnamese Crab Salad with Rice Noodles

SERVES 8-10 AS A STARTER

This is a really gorgeous and substantial salad and I absolutely adore these sweet, salty Southeast Asian flavours.

FOR THE DRESSING:
100g (4oz) sugar, or more to taste
100ml (3½fl oz) fish sauce (nam pla)
100ml (3½fl oz) lemon or lime juice
    (juice of 2 lemons or about 3 limes)
2-3 small chillies, deseeded and
    sliced finely
4 garlic cloves, peeled and crushed
1 tbsp finely grated ginger

FOR THE SALAD:
250g (9oz) thin or medium rice noodles,
150g (5oz) peanuts
450g (1lb) cooked crab meat
1 large cucumber, chopped
300g (11oz) radishes, trimmed and
    sliced
4 tbsp roughly chopped fresh coriander
    leaves and stalks

To make the dressing, mix all the ingredients in a jug. Put the noodles in a bowl of boiling water for 5 minutes until they have softened. Drain and rinse. Meanwhile, toast the peanuts under a grill preheated to hot. Rub off the skins and roughly chop the nuts.

In a bowl, toss together the dressing with the noodles, then add the crabmeat, chopped cucumber and sliced radishes. Sprinkle over the toasted peanuts and the coriander and serve.

VARIATION
CRUNCHY VIETNAMESE SALAD WITH RICE NOODLES
Replace the crab with 100g (4oz) each of bean sprouts, cress and grated carrot.

Sicilian Pasta

SERVES 16–20 / VEGETARIAN

I first tasted this when a friend, James Folks, made it for a group of us, sitting outside on a hot summer's day drinking Prosecco, and it was absolutely divine. It is essential to make the marinade at least 2 hours in advance so that the vegetables almost soften and the flavours infuse.

FOR THE MARINADE:
4 large handfuls torn fresh basil
16 celery stalks, trimmed and finely chopped
16 garlic cloves, peeled and chopped
20 ripe tomatoes, chopped, or 40 cherry tomatoes, quartered
150ml (5fl oz) olive oil
600g (1lb 6oz) buffalo mozzarella, finely chopped
Sea salt and freshly ground black pepper

FOR THE PASTA:
1.8g (4lb) small pasta shapes, such as fusilli

Place all the marinade ingredients in a bowl and season to taste. Leave to sit for at least 2 hours or longer if possible; do not put it in the fridge.

Once the marinade is ready, cook the pasta in a large pot of salted water and drain. Immediately toss with the marinade ingredients – the mozzarella will just begin to melt. Tip into a large serving bowl and place in the middle of the table. This dish is best eaten just warm.

Pasta with Garlic, Anchovies and Breadcrumbs
SERVES 12-15

This very simple peasant pasta dish originates from Naples. It's quick and very delicious.

175g (6oz) breadcrumbs
250ml (9fl oz) olive oil
2 tsp dried chilli flakes
2 x 50g cans anchovy fillets, drained
   and roughly chopped

1 head garlic, separated into cloves,
   peeled and roughly chopped
2kg (4¹/₄lb) spaghetti or tagliatelle
Juice of 1 lemon

Put the breadcrumbs in a dry frying pan and toss over a medium to high heat for a minute or two until they are golden, then set aside. Place the olive oil, chilli flakes, anchovies and garlic in the frying pan over a medium to high heat for about 30 seconds (just long enough for the garlic to lose its rawness). Take off the heat and throw in the breadcrumbs to stop it cooking any more, and set aside.

Cook the pasta in a pot of boiling salted water, until al dente, then drain, leaving a couple of tablespoons of the cooking water in with the pasta. Toss the pasta with the garlic, anchovies and breadcrumbs. Add lemon juice, to taste, toss and serve.

Peas with Leeks
SERVES 12-15

This is a great dish for lots of people as it is so quick to put together.

4 tbsp olive oil
3 leeks, finely sliced
6-8 rashers streaky bacon, finely
   chopped

900g (2lb) peas (can be frozen)
200ml (7fl oz) vegetable (or chicken)
   stock
Salt and freshly ground black pepper

Heat the oil, cook the leeks and streaky bacon over a high heat for 1-2 minutes. Add the peas, stock and seasoning. Bring up to the boil and simmer for 2-3 minutes or until the peas are cooked.

Garlic and Mustard Potatoes

SERVES 12-15 / VEGETARIAN

The flavour of the Dijon mustard goes beautifully with the garlic in this recipe and is the perfect potato dish for large parties.

25g (1oz) butter, softened, plus extra
   for greasing
1.8kg (4lb) peeled potatoes,
   sliced 5mm (1/4in) thick
Salt and freshly ground black pepper
1/2 tsp grated nutmeg

3-4 large garlic cloves, peeled
   and chopped
500ml (18fl oz) double cream
3 tbsp Dijon mustard
75g (3oz) Parmesan cheese,
   finely grated

Preheat the oven to 180°C (350°F), Gas mark 4. Using about 1 teaspoon of butter, butter an ovenproof gratin dish about 25cm (10in) square.

Divide the sliced potatoes into three piles. Place one-third of the potatoes on the base of the dish, season with a pinch of salt, pepper, nutmeg and half the chopped garlic, and dot with butter. Then add another layer of potatoes, season the same way, add the remaining garlic, then add a third layer of potatoes and season again.

Heat the cream in a saucepan, stir in the mustard, and pour over the potatoes; it should come just over halfway up the sides of the dish. Scatter with the finely grated Parmesan, cover with foil and place in the oven for 1 1/4–1 1/2 hours. Remove the foil after 30 minutes. The potatoes should be soft and the top should be golden, with the cream bubbling up the sides of the dish.

RACHEL'S HANDY TIP

If this needs to sit and keep warm in the oven for 30 minutes or so, cover it to prevent it drying out.

Rhubarb, Plum and Cardamom Crumble

SERVES 8-10 / VEGETARIAN

Another lovely recipe from my friend, Iona Murray. This rich, sweet and perfumed crumble is perfect for entertaining as it can be made in advance. It's also great for large parties as all you have to do is multiply the quantities by two or three.

FOR THE FILLING:
50g (2oz) butter
125g (4½oz) brown sugar
400g (14oz) rhubarb, washed and
   sliced into 1cm (½in) pieces
8-12 dark red plums, quartered,
   de-stoned and washed
1 tbsp runny honey
6-8 cardamom pods
1 cinnamon stick, broken in half

1 strip of lemon peel (using a potato
   peeler, peel one strip of the lemon
   zest from top to bottom)
FOR THE TOPPING:
300g (11oz) plain flour
75g (3oz) light brown sugar
2 tsp ground cinnamon
200g (7oz) butter, melted
Approx 1 tbsp sugar, for scattering
   on top

Preheat the oven to 180°C (350°F), Gas mark 4. Melt the butter for the filling in a saucepan and stir in the brown sugar. Then add the rhubarb and plums and a tablespoon of water. Mix, add the honey, cardamom, cinnamon and lemon peel, and cook for about 5 minutes, stirring regularly but gently.

Meanwhile, make the topping. Mix together the dry ingredients and add the melted butter, mixing quickly but lightly to form a crumbly texture. Set aside.

Remove the broken cinnamon stick and lemon peel from the fruit mixture and discard. Pour the mixture into a pie dish, then lightly scatter the crumble mixture on top. Do not press down or it will sink and form a mush. Scatter a tablespoon of sugar on top. Cook in the oven for 20-25 minutes or until the top is golden brown and the juices are bubbling up the side. Serve with softly whipped cream or vanilla ice cream.

VARIATION
The topping mixture is also delicious with a good handful of chopped toasted walnuts, hazelnuts or toasted almonds added.

Toffee, Apple and Almond Crumble

SERVES 12 / VEGETARIAN

This has to be one of my favourite desserts – it's completely divine. The toffee sauce keeps for months in the fridge – so handy for a quick sweet treat. It's great with ice cream and baked bananas too. I usually make twice this recipe, so that I have some left over to store in the fridge.

FOR THE TOFFEE SAUCE:
250g (9oz) golden syrup
250g (9oz) light brown sugar
100g (4oz) butter
200ml (7fl oz) single cream
2 tsp vanilla extract

FOR THE CRUMBLE:
350g (12oz) self-raising flour
Finely grated zest of 2 lemons
150g (5oz) butter, chopped or cubed

175g (6oz) light brown sugar
100g (4oz) ground almonds

FOR THE FILLING:
12 eating apples, peeled, quartered, cored and cut into 2cm (3/4in) chunks
50g (2oz) butter

TO SERVE:
Softly whipped cream, vanilla ice cream or Crème Anglaise (see page 221)

Preheat the oven to 180°C (350°F), Gas mark 4. Put all the ingredients for the toffee sauce into a saucepan over a medium heat and boil for 2–3 minutes, stirring regularly until smooth. Set aside.

Next, make the crumble topping. Place the flour and lemon zest in a bowl, rub in the 150g (5oz) of butter, leaving it a little rough and uneven. Stir in the sugar and ground almonds. Place the crumble in the fridge until you are ready to use it.

To make the filling, melt the 50g (2oz) of butter in a wide saucepan or frying pan, add the chopped apples and toss on the heat for a few minutes until the apples start to soften. Add 125ml (4fl oz) of the toffee sauce (about half; keep the rest for serving) and continue to simmer for a few minutes longer until the apples are just cooked.

Pour into two 1.25 litre (2¼ pint) pie dishes. Sprinkle the crumble over the top and place in the preheated oven for 20–30 minutes, or until the crumble is light golden and with toffee sauce juices bubbling up the sides. Serve warm with softly whipped cream and a jug of the remaining warm toffee sauce.

Lemon and Ginger Ice Cream

SERVES 12 / VEGETARIAN

This is such a delicious, light, one-step ice cream – and you don't need an ice-cream machine to make it. Leave out the ginger if you prefer.

400ml (14fl oz) cool Lemon Curd
  (see page 186)
600ml (20fl oz) natural yoghurt

600ml (20fl oz) crème fraîche
4 tbsp finely grated ginger

Fold together the lemon curd, yoghurt, crème fraîche and ginger and place in the freezer for a few hours until frozen.

VARIATION

LEMON AND GINGER PUDDING

This is a very quick and easy pudding to make. Make exactly as above, but do not freeze! Serve with Lemon Biscuits (see page 45).

9 Edible Gifts

There is something really lovely
about giving and receiving gifts
that have been made by hand,
and all the better if you can eat them!
They're a thoughtful alternative to
the usual bottle of wine when going
to someone's house for dinner, or as
a thank-you present, or a Christmas
gift. Jams, chutneys, preserves,
biscuits, chocolates and fudge can
all look so pretty when packaged
nicely in lovely jars or bags tied up
with ribbon. It's a friendly finishing
touch to make your own labels, too –
you can be as creative as you wish,
and always be sure to include how
best to store your gift, and how
long it should keep.

Cucumber Pickle

MAKES ABOUT 4 X 400G (14OZ) JARS / VEGETARIAN

Mrs Allen started making this at Ballymaloe over 30 years ago and it is one of the handiest recipes to have in your repertoire. Not only is it good for burgers and all kinds of sandwiches, but it is wonderful with cold sliced meats and smoked fish, and it transforms a humble hard-boiled egg and a chunk of Cheddar into a meal. It is a true pickle, so even though it will lose its vibrant green colour, it will keep for weeks and weeks and weeks . . .

900g (2lb) unpeeled cucumber, thinly sliced
3 small onions, peeled and thinly sliced (optional)
350g (12oz) sugar
1 tbsp salt
225ml (7¹/₂fl oz) cider vinegar or white wine vinegar

Mix the cucumber and onion in a large bowl, add the sugar, salt and vinegar, and mix well to combine.

Make 1 hour ahead, if possible, and store in a jar or bowl in the fridge.

Preserved Roasted Peppers with Basil

MAKES 1 MEDIUM-SIZED JAR / VEGETARIAN

I adore having some good roast peppers in the fridge, ready to eat as part of a salad or a Market Plate (see page 214), to throw on top of some freshly cooked pasta, or in a sandwich, or whatever takes your fancy! These make a lovely gift potted into a pretty jar and topped up with olive oil.

4 peppers of various colours, left whole
Olive oil
Basil leaves

Preheat the oven to 230°C (450°F), Gas mark 8. Rub some olive oil over the peppers, then pop on a baking tray in the oven. Cook for about 40 minutes, or until very soft and a little blackened. Take them out of the oven, put into a bowl, cover with cling film and leave to cool.

Once the peppers are cool enough to handle, take them out of the bowl and use your fingers to peel off the skin and break the peppers into quarters. Do not rinse in water or you'll lose the flavour. Then, using a butter knife, scrape the seeds away, which should leave just the flesh. Layer in a sterilised jar (see below), adding basil leaves between the peppers, and fill up with olive oil.

RACHEL'S HANDY TIP
To sterilise jars, either put them through a cycle in your dishwasher, boil them for 5 minutes in a pan of water or place in an oven preheated to 150°C (300°F), Gas mark 2 for 10 minutes.

Tomato, Ginger and Chilli Jam

MAKES 2 X 400G (14OZ) JARS / VEGETARIAN

This is a gorgeous, sweet preserve and makes a great gift. It's really versatile – you can enjoy it with everything from cheese and sausages to roast chicken and cold meats.

50g (2oz) ginger, peeled and chopped
4 large garlic cloves, peeled
4 red chillies
25ml (1fl oz) fish sauce (nam pla)
750g (1¹/₂lb) tomatoes or cherry tomatoes, peeled (see below) and chopped
400g (14oz) sugar
150ml (5fl oz) red wine vinegar

Put the ginger, garlic, chillies and fish sauce into a blender and whiz to purée. Place the purée in a saucepan with the tomatoes, sugar and vinegar and bring to the boil. Stir and simmer, uncovered, for about 40 minutes, stirring regularly until thick and jammy. Pour into sterilised jars (see page 177), cover, and allow to cool.

RACHEL'S HANDY TIP
To peel tomatoes, cut a cross in the skin at the base of the tomato and cover with boiling water for 30 seconds. Remove carefully from the hot water and, holding the tomato in a clean tea towel, slip the skins off. If the skins do not come away easily, return to the hot water for another 30 seconds or so.

Spicy Tomato and Apple Chutney

MAKES ABOUT 4 X 400G (14OZ) JARS / VEGETARIAN

A beautiful little jar of this chutney makes a perfect gift. If possible, it is best left to mature for 1–2 weeks before eating.

1kg (2$^{1}/_{4}$lb) ripe tomatoes, peeled (see page 178) and chopped
2 onions, peeled and chopped
100g (4oz) raisins or sultanas
1 large cooking apple, peeled, cored and roughly chopped
300g (11oz) sugar
225ml (7$^{1}/_{2}$fl oz) white wine vinegar
2 tsp salt
$^{1}/_{2}$ tsp allspice
$^{1}/_{2}$ tsp ground ginger
$^{1}/_{2}$ tsp freshly ground black pepper
$^{1}/_{2}$ tsp cayenne pepper

Place all the ingredients in a stainless-steel saucepan and bring up to the boil, stirring. Continue to simmer over a low heat, uncovered, stirring regularly to make sure the bottom does not burn, for about 1 hour or until it is thick and pulpy. Pour into hot, sterilised jars (see page 177) and cover while the chutney is still hot.

Spiced Cranberry and Orange Relish

MAKES ABOUT 2 X 400G (14OZ) JARS / VEGETARIAN

A perfect Christmas gift! It will keep for weeks and weeks in a sterilised jar.

340g (11¾oz) cranberries, fresh or frozen
1 large pinch of ground cinnamon
1 large pinch of ground ginger
Finely grated zest and juice of 1 large orange
175g (6oz) light muscovado sugar

Place the cranberries (no need to defrost if they are frozen), cinnamon, ginger and the orange juice in a small saucepan and cook over a low heat, with the lid on, stirring regularly, for about 6–7 minutes, until the cranberries have burst. Take off the heat and stir in the grated orange zest and the sugar. Pour into sterilised jars (see page 177).

Onion Marmalade

MAKES 2-3 X 400G (14OZ) JARS / VEGETARIAN

This is a great preserve to give as a gift since it's so versatile. It goes beautifully with cheese, pâtés and cold meats and is perfect with lamb chops or in a steak sandwich too. The marmalade keeps well in a sterilised jar for months.

25g (1oz) butter
675g (1¹/₂lb) onions, peeled and thinly sliced
150g (5oz) caster sugar
1 tsp salt
1 tsp freshly ground black pepper
100ml (3¹/₂fl oz) sherry vinegar, or balsamic vinegar
250ml (8fl oz) full-bodied red wine (it doesn't matter if it has been sitting around for a few days)
2 tbsp crème de cassis (a blackcurrant liqueur)

Melt the butter in the saucepan and add the onions, sugar, salt and freshly ground pepper. Stir, then cover the saucepan and cook for 30 minutes over a gentle heat, stirring from time to time to prevent it from sticking to the bottom of the pan.

Remove the lid and add the vinegar, wine and crème de cassis and cook, uncovered, for another 30 minutes, stirring every now and then. It should be slightly thick by now. Pour into sterilised jars (see page 177) and cover while hot. It will thicken as it cools.

Summer Fruit Jam

MAKES 2 X 400G (14OZ) JARS / VEGETARIAN

People always think you are a genius if you make jam, but it really couldn't be easier. So, impress your friends with jammy gifts! If you are going to double this recipe, make sure you use a suitably large saucepan.

400g (14oz) sugar
400g (14oz) summer fruit – a mixture of strawberries, raspberries, redcurrants, blackcurrants, blackberries and blueberries (you can use frozen fruits out of season)
Juice of 1 lemon

Place the sugar in a heatproof bowl and pop in a moderate oven for 10 minutes to heat up. You can also place the jars into the oven to warm, to prevent them cracking when the hot jam is poured into them.

Put a saucer in the freezer for testing the jam later on.

Place the fruit (which can be frozen) in a saucepan with the lemon juice and heat up. Simmer for 3 minutes and crush most of the fruit with a potato masher. Add the warm sugar, stir to dissolve and bring up to the boil. Boil for 3–4 minutes over a high heat, stirring regularly.

To test to see if the jam is cooked, take a spoonful of the jam, place it on the frozen plate and allow it to sit for a few seconds. Then push your finger through the blob of jam – if the skin on top forms a wrinkle when pushed, it is cooked. Remove from the heat immediately and pour into sterilised jars (see page 177) or a bowl. A jam funnel is handy for this if you have one. Place the lids on top. The jam will set as it cools.

Orange, Lemon and Grapefruit Marmalade

MAKES ABOUT 2.5KG (5¹/₂LB) OR 7 JARS / VEGETARIAN

There are certain mornings when all I feel like having for breakfast is a nice cup of tea and toast with really good marmalade. This particular recipe is made in the same no-fuss way that my grandpa makes his.

2 oranges
2 grapefruit
2 lemons
Water to cover the fruit plus 1 litre (1¾ pints)
1.25kg (2¹/₂lb) sugar

Place all the fruit in a large saucepan, cover with water and boil for 1 hour until soft. The lemons may cook slightly faster, so check after 45 minutes and, if soft, remove them while the other fruit finishes cooking.

Take the pan off the heat, discard the cooking water and allow the fruit to cool for a few minutes. Cut the fruit into quarters, then use a spoon to scrape out the pulp, discarding the pips. Place the pulp in a food processor or liquidiser. If you don't want peel in your marmalade, add the peel to the liquidiser, too. Add 50ml (2fl oz) of the 1 litre (1¾ pints) of water and whiz until fine, then push through a sieve into a large saucepan. Add the remainder of the water. If you do want peel in your marmalade, cut the peel into fine slices (or more roughly if you want chunky marmalade) and add to the saucepan.

Bring up to the boil and boil rapidly, uncovered, for 10 minutes stirring every now and then. Add the sugar, stir until it dissolves, then boil over a high heat for 10 minutes.

Meanwhile, place a saucer in the fridge or freezer. When the marmalade has boiled for 10 minutes, place a blob of the marmalade on the chilled plate and then chill for 1 minute. Push your finger through the blob – if the skin on top forms a wrinkle when pushed, it is cooked. If it is not ready, continue boiling it until it is cooked – this may take up to another 10 minutes, depending on the pectin levels in the fruit. When it is cooked, remove from the heat and pour into sterilised jars (see page 177).

Rhubarb and Ginger Jam

MAKES 3-4 X 400G (14OZ) JARS / VEGETARIAN

I adore this jam – the subtle flavour of the ginger is great with the rhubarb, and it is very quick and easy to make.

900g (2lb) rhubarb, trimmed and sliced
900g (2lb) sugar
100ml (3¹/₂fl oz) water
3 tbsp finely grated ginger
75ml (2³/₄fl oz) lemon juice (juice of 2 large or 3 small lemons)

Place a saucer in the freezer. Place all the ingredients in a large saucepan over a medium heat and stir until the sugar dissolves. Turn up the heat, bring to the boil and boil rapidly for 15 minutes until cooked. To test to see if the jam is cooked, take the saucer from the freezer and pour a teaspoon of jam onto it. If a wrinkle forms on the top when you push your finger through the blob, the jam is cooked. Pour into sterilised jars (see page 177) and cover while still hot.

Lemon Curd

MAKES 1 X 400G (14OZ) JAR / VEGETARIAN

My aunt, Gay, gave me a lovely big jar full of the most delicious lemon curd for Christmas. It kept me going for weeks – spreading it on toast and drop scones, enjoying it with meringues and cream, and then finally making it into Lemon and Ginger Ice Cream (see page 171). Delicious!

2 eggs
1 egg yolk
100g (4oz) butter
175g (6oz) caster sugar
Finely grated zest and juice of 3 lemons

Beat the whole eggs and extra egg yolk together. Melt the butter in a saucepan over a very low heat. Add the caster sugar, grated zest and lemon juice and then the beaten eggs. Stir carefully over a very gentle heat until the mixture thickens. This may take about 10 minutes. If the heat is too high, the eggs will scramble.

When the mixture is thick enough to coat the back of a spoon and leave a clear mark when you push your finger through it, the curd is cooked ready.

Remove from the heat and pour into a sterilised jar (see page 177). Allow to cool, then place in the fridge for up to 2 weeks.

Dark Chocolate and Stem Ginger Biscuits

MAKES ABOUT 25 BISCUITS / VEGETARIAN

These are gorgeous, intensely flavoured little shortbread biscuits. Serve them with coffee or pop them into a bag and tie it up with a ribbon for a perfect present.

150g (5oz) plain flour
25g (1oz) rice flour (if you do not have rice flour, use 175g (6oz) plain flour,
    although the rice flour gives a lovely crumbly texture)
125g (4¹/₂oz) butter, softened
50g (2oz) light brown sugar
75g (3oz) crystallised ginger, finely chopped
75g (3oz) dark chocolate, chopped

Preheat the oven to 180°C (350°F), Gas mark 4. Place the flours, butter, sugar, and ginger in a food processor and whiz to combine – if you do not have a food processor, cream the butter and add in the other ingredients, mixing with a wooden spoon until they form a dough.

Roll the dough into balls the size of large cherry tomatoes and place on a baking tray (no need to grease or line). Using a wet fork, flatten each one slightly and cook in the preheated oven for 8–12 minutes, or until golden and firm. Remove carefully from the tray and cool on a wire rack.

Melt the chocolate gently in a warm oven, a microwave or in a bowl sitting over a saucepan of simmering water. Allow to cool slightly, then use a pastry brush or a butter knife to spread the cooked biscuits with the melted chocolate or dip the top of the biscuits into the melted chocolate and allow the chocolate to cool and set.

Chocolate Praline Truffles

MAKES ABOUT 40 / VEGETARIAN

These are rich and delicious after-dinner truffles that are well worth the effort of making. They are an impressive gift – who wouldn't love them? For these you need to make praline in which to roll the truffles, but you could always roll them in cocoa powder too. Praline is a lovely, indulgent staple to have on hand in the kitchen. Try sprinkling on top of the Toffee Sundae on page 31.

FOR THE PRALINE:
100g (4oz) caster sugar
100g (4oz) unpeeled almonds
FOR THE TRUFFLES:
150ml (5fl oz) single cream
225g (8oz) dark chocolate, chopped
1 tbsp whiskey or rum (optional)

First, make the praline. Put a sheet of greaseproof paper on a baking tray. Place the sugar and almonds in a saucepan or a non-stick frying pan over a medium heat. Allow the sugar to caramelise slowly; do not stir the mixture, but you can swirl the pan if it is browning unevenly. Cook until all the sugar has caramelised to a rich golden brown (the colour of whiskey). Pour the mixture onto the parchment paper and allow to cool completely; it will harden as it cools.

When it is cool, whiz it up in a food processor or place in a plastic bag and bash it with a rolling pin – you want it to become the texture of breadcrumbs. Store in a covered box or jar until you need it; it will keep for a month like this.

To make the truffles, place the cream in a saucepan and bring up to the boil, add the chocolate and the whiskey or rum, if using. Stir until the chocolate has melted and the mixture is smooth. Pour into a shallow pie dish and allow to cool and set. Then either roll into balls with wet hands (nice messy work!) or scoop up with a melon baller or teaspoon (keep dipping it into hot water for easier scooping). Drop into a bowl of praline and toss to cover the chocolates in the crunchy nutty coating. Serve with coffee after dinner.

Heavenly Fudge

MAKES ABOUT 60 PIECES / VEGETARIAN

I adore this fudge – it's sweet, a little bit crumbly and creamy, and oh so hard to resist. It only takes 20 minutes to make from start to finish. My sister, Simone, and I used to make fudge with Mum when we were little, and I still make it now.

1 x 375g tin of condensed milk
100g (4oz) butter
450g (1lb) caster or muscovado sugar

Place the condensed milk, butter and sugar in a saucepan. Stir and bring to the boil. Boil for about 10 minutes, stirring all the time (do not let it burn on the bottom) until it reaches the soft ball stage. To test for this, put a 1/2 teaspoon blob of the fudge into a bowl of cold water – it should be firm but malleable.

Remove from the heat and sit the bottom of the saucepan in a bowl of cold water that comes 2–3cm (3/4–1 1/4in) up the outside of the pan. Stir until the fudge cools down a bit – it will go from smooth, shiny and toffeeish, to looking matt in appearance, thick and grainy.

Scrape the contents of the saucepan into a square cake tin 20 x 20cm (8 x 8in) or to cover about two-thirds of a small Swiss roll tin or baking tray. The fudge should be 1–1.5cm (1/2–3/4in) thick. Let it cool, then cut into squares.

VARIATIONS

VANILLA FUDGE
Add 1 teaspoon of vanilla extract or essence to the ingredients at the start.

CHOCOLATE FUDGE
Add 75g (3oz) dark chocolate (with 70% cocoa solids if possible), chopped, to the fudge when you take it off the heat. Stir to melt the chocolate before placing in the bowl of cold water.

Sinful Butterscotch

MAKES ABOUT 24 PIECES / VEGETARIAN

My dentist would not approve of this, but I secretly love it! I'd be happy to receive this as a gift any time . . .

400g (14oz) sugar
200ml (7fl oz) water
100g (4oz) powdered glucose (available in chemists)
100g (4oz) butter
½ tsp salt

Line an 18 x 24cm (7 x 9½in) tin with greaseproof paper.

Combine the sugar, water and glucose in a saucepan. Stir over a low heat until the sugar is dissolved, bring to the boil and boil for about 15 minutes or until the mixture is light golden brown. Remove from the heat, immediately add the butter and salt, and stir until well blended. Pour into the prepared tin. Mark into squares while still hot. The butterscotch will harden as it cools. Break into pieces.

Vanilla Melting Moments
MAKES 20 / VEGETARIAN

These light, crumbly little biscuits literally do melt in your mouth and are absolutely divine.

FOR THE BISCUITS:
175g (6oz) self-raising flour
125g (4¹/₂oz) cornflour
50g (2oz) icing sugar
225g (8oz) butter, cut into pieces
1 tsp vanilla essence

FOR THE VANILLA BUTTER ICING:
50g (2oz) butter, softened
125g (4¹/₂oz) icing sugar, plus extra
   to dust
¹/₂ tsp vanilla essence

Preheat the oven to 160°C (325°F), Gas mark 3. Place the self-raising flour, cornflour and icing sugar in a food processor and whiz for a second. Add the butter and vanilla essence and mix until it comes together. Roll the mixture into small balls the size of a large marble, and place on a baking tray (no need to line) with a little space in between them. Dip a fork in cold water and press down on each one to flatten slightly and score.

Bake for 10–15 minutes until still very pale in colour but slightly firm. Remove carefully from the tray and allow to cool on a wire rack.

Meanwhile, make the butter icing. (I usually make this in the food processor bowl in which I have just mixed the biscuit dough.) Mix all the ingredients until they come together. Keep at room temperature to remain soft.

When the biscuits have cooled, place a butter knife in a cup of boiling water and use the warm, damp knife to spread the icing on one half (take care not to break the biscuits). Sandwich with another half. Dust with icing sugar.

RACHEL'S HANDY TIP
If you do not have a food processor, just rub the butter and vanilla into the dry ingredients in a bowl, then work with your hands until it comes together.

VARIATION
Make single biscuits and brush with approximately 75g (3oz) melted chocolate. Top with small pieces of chopped crystallised ginger.

10 Just Like Mum Used To Make

There are times when we all need something really comforting to eat; food that is warming, wholesome, old-fashioned and hearty, with a hint of nostalgia. Chunky soups, gooey cheese fondue, great bangers and mash, Mum's macaroni cheese, and a butterscotch pudding will all help to beat the blues on a cold winter's day. This kind of food should be fairly easy and straightforward to make, and will even transport well to the sofa for those times when all you want to do is curl up under a blanket.

Homemade Pork Sausages with Colcannon and Apple Sauce

SERVES 4 (MAKES ABOUT 12)

For me there is nothing quite so comforting as bangers and mash, and these homemade sausages are ever so tasty and easy to make. They have no casing so are made in a flash, and are great for children and adults, alike. Colcannon, which is a traditional Halloween-time Irish mashed potato with cabbage, is perfect winter food. I also love to serve this colcannon with Pork Chops with Caramelised Apples (see page 202).

FOR THE SAUSAGES:
450g (1lb) fatty minced pork
50g (2oz) breadcrumbs
1 egg, whisked
1 garlic clove, peeled and crushed
1 tbsp chopped fresh parsley
   or marjoram
3 tbsp olive or sunflower oil
Salt and freshly ground black pepper

FOR THE COLCANNON:
1.5kg (3lb) floury potatoes, scrubbed
100g (4oz) butter
500g (1lb 2oz) green cabbage, outer
   leaves removed
250ml (8fl oz) hot milk
2 tbsp chopped parsley
FOR THE APPLE SAUCE:
1 large cooking apple (350g (12oz)),
   peeled, cored and roughly chopped
1 tbsp water
25-50g (1-2oz) caster sugar

For the sausages, mix together all the ingredients, except the olive oil, and season with salt and pepper. Fry a tiny bit of the mixture in a pan with a little olive or sunflower oil to see if the seasoning is good.

Divide the mixture into 12 pieces and shape each one into a sausage. Place on a baking tray or plate and set aside until you want to cook them. (Chilling them for a day in the fridge is fine, or you can freeze them.)

To make the colcannon, cook the potatoes in boiling salted water until tender, draining three-quarters of the water after 5–10 minutes and continuing to cook over a low heat. Avoid stabbing the potatoes with a knife as this will make them break up. When cooked, drain all the remaining water, peel and mash with 50g

(2oz) of the butter while hot. I usually hold the potato on a fork and peel with a knife if they are hot.

Meanwhile, cook the cabbage. Cut the cabbage into quarters, then cut out the core. Slice the cabbage finely across the grain. Heat a saucepan, add the remaining butter, 2 tbsp water and the sliced cabbage. Toss over a medium heat for 5–7 minutes, until just cooked. Add to the potatoes, then add the hot milk and the parsley, keeping some of the milk back in case you do not need it all. Season to taste and beat until creamy and smooth, adding more milk if necessary. Serve piping hot with the remaining butter melting in the centre.

To make the apple sauce, place the apple in a small saucepan with the water. Put the lid on and cook over a gentle heat (stir every now and then) until the apple has broken down to a mush. Add sugar to taste. Serve warm or at room temperature.

To cook the sausages, heat a frying pan on a low to medium heat, add 2 tablespoons of olive or sunflower oil and gently fry the sausages for 12–15 minutes, until golden on all sides and cooked on the inside. Serve with the colcannon and apple sauce.

RACHEL'S HANDY TIP
To make breadcrumbs, just put a slice of slightly stale bread (with or without crusts) in a food processor or liquidiser and whiz.

VARIATIONS
The sausage mixture is also delicious shaped into little balls and used instead of the minced beef for Meatballs with Fresh Tomato Sauce (see page 82).

SPICY SAUSAGES WITH CORIANDER
Replace the herbs with 2 tablespoons chopped coriander, and add half a deseeded, chopped red chilli or a pinch of dried chilli flakes and serve with sweet chilli sauce or Tomato, Ginger and Chilli Jam (see page 178).

Baked Eggs and Soldiers
SERVES 6 / VEGETARIAN

These always remind me of when I was little, as we would often have them for an easy brunch or for a late supper.

6 eggs
6 tbsp single cream
Salt and freshly ground black pepper
15g (1/2oz) butter, divided into 6 knobs
Bread, for toasting

Preheat the oven to 160°C (325°F), Gas mark 3. Bring the kettle to the boil. Break each of the eggs into a ramekin dish, add 1 tablespoon of cream to each and then top with a knob of butter and a pinch of salt and pepper. Place the ramekins in a roasting tin, pour boiling water into the tray so that it comes about halfway up the sides of the dishes and place carefully into the preheated oven. Bake the eggs for 10 minutes or until the eggs are almost set.

Toast some bread until golden, butter it and cut into soldiers (fingers). Serve the baked eggs with hot buttered soldiers on the side.

RACHEL'S HANDY TIP
Try dipping cooked asparagus spears (see page 98) into baked eggs for a sophisticated supper treat.

Chunky Mediterranean Pasta Soup

SERVES 6

This is a gorgeously gutsy soup – definitely a meal in itself. It's the best thing (apart from a sunny beach holiday) for beating the winter blues!

2 tbsp olive oil
250g (9oz) chorizo, chopped into 1cm (1/2in) chunks
1 large onion, peeled and chopped
4 large garlic cloves, peeled and crushed
Salt and freshly ground black pepper
2 x 400g tins chopped tomatoes (or 900g (2lb) fresh tomatoes, peeled (see page 178) and chopped)
900ml (1¹/₂ pints) chicken stock

2 tbsp chopped herbs – I like to use a mixture of rosemary, thyme and parsley
Pinch of sugar (optional)
250g (9oz) dried pasta, such as orzo or fusilli
150g (5oz) shredded spinach or whole baby spinach leaves

TO SERVE:
Freshly grated Parmesan cheese
Small bowl of Classic Basil Pesto (see page 217)

Heat the olive oil in a large saucepan, add the chorizo and cook for 2 minutes. Add the chopped onion and garlic and season, then sweat over a gentle heat for 7–8 minutes, until soft. Add the tomatoes, stock and herbs, if necessary season again with salt, pepper and a good pinch of sugar, and simmer with the lid on for another 10 minutes or until the tomatoes are soft.

Add the pasta and continue to simmer for another 6–10 minutes, stirring regularly or until the pasta is cooked. When you are ready to serve, drop in the spinach and boil for just 1 minute or until the spinach is wilted. Taste for seasoning. To serve, ladle the chunky soup into large warm bowls and sprinkle with some finely grated Parmesan and a drizzle of pesto.

Pork Chops with Caramelised Apples

SERVES 6

I love this combination of flavours: pork and apples – and cooked like this, they make a perfect supper or big lunch.

2–3 small pork chops per person
Olive oil
Salt and freshly ground black pepper

FOR THE CARAMELISED APPLES:
25g (1oz) butter
3 eating apples, peeled, cored and
    cut into slices 5mm (1/4in) thick
25g (1oz) sugar
Juice of 1/2 lemon

Drizzle the chops with a little olive oil and black pepper. Leave to sit in the fridge until you need to cook them – all day is fine.

Preheat the oven to 190°C (375°F), Gas mark 5. Place a baking tray in the oven to heat up.

To prepare the caramelised apples, heat the butter in a frying pan. Add the apples and the sugar and toss on the heat for 4–5 minutes until cooked and golden. Squeeze in the lemon juice and keep warm.

Heat a frying pan until very hot, then cook the chops in batches, on both sides until golden. Sprinkle with salt, then pop them onto the hot baking tray in the oven and cook for another 5–10 minutes or until cooked through.

Serve the pork chops with the caramelised apples and some Garlic and Mustard Potatoes (see page 167) on the side.

Steak with Blue Cheese Butter and Walnut Salad

SERVES 2

This is serious comfort food and only takes 5 minutes to prepare, which is perfect for those times when you have just come home from work and need some real food fast!

FOR THE STEAKS:
2 sirloin or fillet steaks, excess
   fat removed
A drizzle of olive oil
Sea salt and freshly ground
   black pepper

FOR THE BLUE CHEESE BUTTER:
25g (1oz) blue cheese, rind removed
25g (1oz) butter
Freshly ground black pepper

FOR THE SALAD:
2 handfuls of a mixture of watercress,
   rocket and baby spinach
A drizzle of olive oil (about 1 tbsp)
A small squeeze of lemon juice (about
   1/2–1 tsp)
Sea salt and freshly ground black
   pepper
25g (1oz) chopped walnuts, tossed over
   the heat in a dry pan until golden

Place the pan for the steaks on the heat. Drizzle the steaks with olive oil and sprinkle with black pepper, then allow to sit while the pan heats up.

To make the blue cheese butter, mash together the blue cheese and the butter in a bowl. Add some black pepper, then form into a log and wrap in cling film. Pop in the fridge to cool, or the freezer if you just have a few minutes.

When the pan is very hot, sprinkle the steaks with sea salt and place in the pan. Cook until one side turns a deep golden colour and is seared, then turn over and cook until they are how you like them, 1–2 minutes for rare, about 4 minutes for medium or 8–10 minutes on a lower heat (so they don't burn) for well done. The cooking times will vary depending on the thickness of the steaks and the heat of the pan. When the steaks are cooked, take them off the heat and allow to rest while you toss the salad leaves in the olive oil, lemon juice, sea salt and pepper. Put the steaks on warm plates and top with slices of blue cheese butter. Serve with the dressed leaves sprinkled with chopped walnuts.

Macaroni Cheese

SERVES 6-8 / VEGETARIAN

Macaroni cheese must be the ultimate cure-all for adults and children alike. You can also add small pieces of cooked ham or bacon to the sauce. Macaroni cheese can be made in advance and then reheated when you are ready to serve.

75g (3oz) butter
1 onion, peeled and chopped
75g (3oz) plain flour
900ml (1¹/₂ pints) boiling milk
1-2 tsp Dijon mustard
225g (8oz) cheese (Cheddar, or, even better, half Cheddar and half
    Gruyère), grated
Salt and freshly ground black pepper
300g (11oz) macaroni pasta

Melt the butter in a saucepan, add the chopped onions and cook gently until soft. Stir in the flour and cook for a minute, then gradually add the milk, whisking all the time, and the mustard. Whisk in three-quarters of the cheese and allow to melt into the sauce, then season to taste with salt and pepper.

Cook the pasta in a large pot of boiling water with a teaspoon of salt, until just soft. Drain, then toss into the cheese sauce and transfer into a gratin dish, about 25cm (10in) square. Sprinkle with the remaining cheese and pop under a hot grill for a few minutes to brown the cheese on top, or if you wish, put this aside for later. To reheat, put the dish into an oven preheated to 200°C (400°F), Gas mark 6 for about 25 minutes, or until golden and bubbling.

Oven-baked Risotto with Mushrooms and Thyme

SERVES 4-6 / VEGETARIAN

Risotto goes straight to the heart of both children and adults. You can always leave out the mushrooms if you wish.

Scant 25g (1oz) dried mushrooms, such as porcini or a mixture of types
400ml (14fl oz) boiling water
2 tbsp olive oil
1 small onion, peeled and chopped
2 garlic cloves, peeled and crushed
Salt and freshly ground black pepper

350g (12oz) risotto rice, such as carnaroli or arborio
1 tsp thyme leaves, chopped
750ml (1¼ pints) hot vegetable (or chicken) stock
125ml (4fl oz) white wine
75g (3oz) Parmesan cheese, grated
1 tsp fresh thyme leaves

Preheat the oven to 180°C (350°F), Gas mark 4. Place the dried mushrooms in a bowl, add the boiling water and leave to soak for 10 minutes. Meanwhile, heat the olive oil in a medium ovenproof saucepan or casserole and cook the onion and garlic for a few minutes until soft and a little golden. Season with salt and pepper.

Drain and chop the mushrooms, and reserve the liquid. Add the mushrooms to the garlic and onions with the rice, chopped thyme and the sieved, drained mushroom-soaking liquid. Pour in the stock and wine, bring to the boil and season to taste. Cover with the lid and place in the preheated oven and cook for 15–20 minutes, or until the rice is just cooked and all the liquid has been absorbed. Stir in 50g (2oz) of the grated Parmesan and check the seasoning. To serve, sprinkle with the remaining Parmesan and thyme leaves.

RACHEL'S HANDY TIP
The alcohol in the wine burns off during the cooking of the risotto and the flavour is lovely, but if you do not want to use it, just replace it with extra stock.